WHERE CREDIT IS DUE

Where Credit is Due

*Income-generating programmes for the poor
in developing countries*

JOE REMENYI

IT PUBLICATIONS 1991

Intermediate Technology Publications
103–105 Southampton Row, London WC1B 4HH, UK

The publishers gratefully acknowledge the assistance of the Foundation for Development Co-operation in the publication of this book. The basic aim of the Foundation is to undertake, promote and support activities to improve the quality and increase the quantity of Australian aid to, and co-operation with, developing countries. This includes non-governmental development activities designed to contribute to income generation, job creation, small-enterprise development and other self-help activities at the grassroots level.

ISBN 1 85339 079 8

A CIP catalogue record for this book is available from the British Library

Typeset by Inforum Typesetting, Portsmouth
Printed by BPPC Wheatons, Exeter

Contents

Tables

Figures

Foreword

THIS BOOK IS about poverty in the Third World and what is being done successfully by some of the poor to overcome their plight. It is also about the contribution that people and organizations concerned to help in the alleviation of poverty can make to further that effort and relieve many more people from the degradations of poverty. This book is a record of what is and can be done. It was initiated in response to the deeply felt belief by members of the Oxford Conference on Christian Faith and Economics, an international umbrella body of individuals from diverse backgrounds, that the success of credit-based income-generation programmes in poverty alleviation should be proclaimed wide and far.

The positive results of many of these programmes in generating increased incomes, employment and small enterprises for the poor were briefly reported to a meeting of the Oxford Conference in January 1987. The Conference accordingly appointed a small Project Steering Committee consisting of Dr John Chang of the Asian Development Bank, Mr David Bussau of Maranatha Trust, Dr Bryant Myers of World Vision International and myself to organize and co-ordinate the study.

The Committee outlined the main aim: 'To describe and analyse the role of income generation and wealth creation, as distinct from wealth re-distribution activities, in alleviating human poverty, with particular reference to the role and activities of Christian and other development organizations workiing in this field among the poorest of the poor in developing countries.'

The Committee expressed the hope that the study would serve three primary end-uses and users:

○ to help make qualitative improvements to the work of development organizations (by reporting and analysing the most successful experiences and methods of others in the field)

○ to mobilize additional effort and resources, both public and private, in support of these programmes; and

○ to report back to the Second Oxford Conference, to be held in January 1990.

After an extensive search of suitable candidates, the Project Steering Committee appointed Professor Joe Remenyi, Convener of Development Studies at Deakin University, Geelong, Australia, as its Research Leader. Professor Remenyi has had extensive developing country experience, having worked as a developing country research programme co-ordinator for both the Ford Foundation, 1976–8, and the Australian Centre for International Agricultural Research, 1984–7. I was pleased to be able to accompany Professor Remenyi on many of the field visits undertaken for this study. In so doing, I could only note with admiration the diligence and professional skill with which he pursued his enquiries, and that this was more than matched by the intense interest and genuine compassion which he showed for the true clients of the study — the poor.

Professor Remenyi's study was enthusiastically received by the more than 100 economists, bankers, theologians and development professionals who gathered in Oxford in January 1990. The Conference accepted the main findings of the study and affirmed the urgent need to increase the global commitment to credit-based income-generation programmes by the poor. The participants resolved to commend and promote the value of such programmes to all governments, financial institutions, organizations and individuals concerned with poverty alleviation. The Conference recommended that the study should be published and disseminated worldwide.

My colleagues on the Project Steering Committee join with Professor Remenyi and myself in expressing the hope that this study will contribute to a clearer and better understanding of the nature and extent of human poverty, and of some possible directions in which the poor themselves, as well as those who are more fortunate and concerned in the world community, including the world Christian community, and in the world banking community, may be able to respond to their most urgent plea. This is surely for the kind of help that will enhance human dignity 'by helping the poor to help themselves'.

WILLIAM TAYLOR   Chairman, Steering Committee
Oxford Conference Income-Generation Project   September 1990

Introduction

IN JANUARY 1987, an international meeting was convened at Oxford University, England, to try to develop a better understanding of the relationship between Christian faith and economics. Conferees from across the globe explored the practical applications of this relationship in the modern world. A broad range of backgrounds and professions was represented, including economists, sociologists, philosophers and theologians, as well as business, banking and overseas development specialists. They came from fourteen countries in five continents, covering both developed and developing societies. As a group they reflected widely different socio-political views, disagreed sharply about many things but also found significant areas of agreement.

One such area affecting economic development was, for example, that the promotion of human dignity, 'is a key criterion for evaluating economic systems and structures'. How this agreed principle can be applied in a world characterized by deep divisions between rich and poor did not, however, elicit such ready agreement. The issue was hotly debated. On the one hand were those who place most emphasis upon the need for basic structural change and wealth re-distribution from rich to poor (the redistributionists) as a precondition to successful poverty alleviation; on the other hand were those who place the primary emphasis upon the virtues of self-help for income generation and wealth creation by the poor (the wealth-creationists), as the most practical and sustainable solution to the problem of poverty.

The redistributionists argued their case from the premise that chronic global poverty represents an unjust and unequal distribution of economic wealth and is essentially a structural problem reflecting the skewed ownership of the means of production, distribution and exchange. For them poverty can only be overcome by the introduction of quite fundamental socio-political structural change, such as has been advocated by liberation theologians in Latin America.

There were many redistributionists at the Conference. The wealth-creationists, also a sizeable group, had some sympathy with the redistributionist camp, and welcomed all realistic efforts towards a more just international economic order, such as the current effort within the United Nations to negotiate a reduction in developed country tariffs against developing country exports. They remained sceptical, however, of the ultimate efficacy of such efforts, pursued in isolation from the realities of the daily struggle by the poor to survive, to resolve the problem of global poverty in time to matter for the majority of the world's poor.

The wealth-creationists drew the Conference's attention to the fairly recent and rapidly growing effort of private sector development organizations — the so-called non-government organizations (NGOs) — to support the hitherto largely neglected efforts and potential of the poor to help themselves. Where the redistributionists focused on the 'causes of poverty', the new approach of the wealth-creationists focuses on the 'obstacles to escape from povety'. This frequently takes the form of assistance to 'self-help' organizations in the Third World to develop more effective programmes of income generation, job-creation and small enterprise development at grassroots level. Most of the more successful programmes include a significant component of small-scale revolving credit, to help the poor to help themselves. This book is about these programmes, their impact and why access to credit by the poor is such an essential part of poverty alleviation.

The wealth-creationist view does not reject the need to root out injustices associated with a biased distribution of wealth and income in the world. It accepts that mass absolute poverty implies the denial of justice to the poor. The point of departure is founded on the conviction that, 'one of the most important barriers to development . . . is a belief . . . that the way to get ahead is through the appropriation of existing wealth, not through productive work and investment' (Korten, 1988: 8).

In addition to this important philosophical difference, the proponents of income-generation programmes seek to draw attention to the apparent long-term sterility of 'Robin Hood' type wealth redistribution strategies of development. There is little evidence, whether taken from the study of illegal wealth expropriations or legal wealth redistribution policies, to indicate that they have anything beyond short-term, once-off asset transfer effects and little in the way of sustained positive income and wealth-generation consequences. The struggle for land reform in Asia and Latin America, the expulsion of Asian business-people from Uganda, and the failure of progressive income tax systems to redistribute wealth are three examples that seem to illustrate this in an unequivocal fashion. Similarly, some doubt must surround the relevance of cargo-cult, dole-out policies to the long-term challenge of poverty alleviation in the Third World. A permanent solution to the immediacy and perniciousness of widespead abject poverty requires more than a simple redistribution of existing wealth from the rich to the poor by gratuitous expropriation, or excessive reliance on official social welfare and government-to-government aid.

There is no consensus as to the most important of the many causes of poverty but there is reason to believe that 'involuntary poverty' is primarily the result of events or series of events over which individuals have little control. Natural disasters are important examples, such as the annual floods that devastate Bangladesh each year, droughts such as those that South Asia and Africa experience following the failure of the annual rainy season, earthquakes such as those that have devastated Latin America, the Near East in the Soviet bloc, and the People's Republic of China in recent years. Political upheavals are similarly discombobulating. Wars and revolutions leave a legacy of displaced persons and refugees that have been a key source of growth of numbers in poverty, especially in Africa and Latin America. Events such as these destroy assets that form the protection that rural and urban households rely upon to keep them beyond poverty. Once destroyed they are unable to withstand the next blow of ill-fate, and join the downward spiral into abject poverty. Their problem is not so much that they are now poor, but that processes take hold of their lives that prevent them from helping themselves to escape the state of poverty thrust upon them. The processes that institutionalize poverty and create a class of 'systemic poor' have been well described by Dominique Lapierre (1986) in his international bestseller *The City of Joy*.

The wealth-creationists directed the Conference's attention, therefore, away from the causes of poverty to the need to address the key obstacles to escape from poverty through wealth-creation by the poor. This was presented as a viable and effective alternative, or complement, to redistribution strategies of poverty alleviation. The wealth-creationists asked those at the Conference to focus not on hand-out style welfare strategies, no matter how unjust the current environment, but on what can be done to remove the obstacles that prevent the poor from helping themselves.

In Christian company, concern for the poor is a *sine qua non* of a true follower of Christ, irrespective of whether one is a redistributionist or a creationist. What is lacking is a consensus on what Christians ought to do about poverty as it exists in the developing world and among the marginalized poor who live in the midst of plenty in the industrialized economies. For some Christians it is enough that they pray for the poor. For others something more activist is essential. Among the indigenous Christian institutions of the developing world, there are some that have adopted a grassroots community-development approach to their ministry, dedicated to assisting the poor through income- and employment-generation projects and programmes. These *cognoscenti* heralded their experiences as pointing to viable and effective ways in which non-governmental organizations, including Christian and other religious groups, are making a difference in the fight against systemic poverty. 'Where', asked those unfamiliar with this approach, 'could one find accounts of such efforts?' 'Is there a readily available source where one can read of the experiences of others that their successes may be emulated and supported?' This book has been written in response to that call.

The task of 'documenting and analysing the multiplicity of income-generation project experiences' of Christian and other NGOs in the Third World is a daunting prospect; one that is impossible without some strict definitional boundaries. The project began, therefore, by setting some limits. We were not in a position to examine the universe of relevant activities, for both the time-frame available and the budget constraints were severe. After much consultation and discussion it was decided to confine research for the book to programmes that:

○ are income- and employment-generation initiatives of NGOs rather than governments

- have a reputation for success, confirmed by a review of available annual and independent evaluation reports
- incorporate a credit component, typically a revolving credit fund, to address the finance constraint confronting individuals and microenterprise activities of members
- operate essentially at the lower end of the economic scale (i.e., in the 'informal sector'), with a policy favouring small loans (i.e., often less than $100), of short duration (typically less than twelve months), for productive purposes, (i.e., income- and employment-generating, non-consumption); and
- seek to work through the private sector to develop greater self-reliance and a more favourable environment for small business development of benefit to the poor.

The three key parameters that define the domain of this study are, therefore, the private-sector focus of the development projects examined, the targetting of so called 'micro-enterprises', and the provision of credit-finance to fund enterprise creation and business expansion.

There are many ways other than the provision of credit in which 'income- and employment-generation' goals can be pursued by NGOs in the Third World: some NGOs concentrate on literacy and skills training in order to expand the range of economic opportunities open to the people with whom they work; other programmes follow an integrated 'primary health-care' strategy, targetted at women and children in particular, in order to reduce morbidity and raise household productivity; the more radical programmes adopt methods that seek to empower the poor by raising their awareness of ways in which they might break out of the oppression that is the source of their poverty. Such 'liberation' programmes can involve heated confrontation with those in whose interests it might be to retain the status quo.

The programmes examined in this book have not, in the main, followed these alternative paths to income and employment generation. Why have we eschewed them in favour of those that are best described as 'credit-based income-generation projects' (CIGPs)? The answer lies in our belief that these important and legitimate ways of working with the poor are not 'key logs in the sustainable development jam' in the unique way in which the denial of access to investment finance is crucial. In order to understand why this is so, we must turn our attention to the daily realities obvious to the poor but elusive to all who ignore the simple economics of survival in the world of the poor.

The study begins, therefore, with a closer look at the anatomy of poverty and what it means to be poor in the Third World. It is both a description and an analysis of the record achieved by some successful pioneers in 'development for the poor by the poor'. Each of these pioneers is from the non-government, private sector, usually a not-for-profit or welfare-oriented NGO associated with 'grassroots' micro-enterprise promotion and support. Each of the programmes examined has in common the use of various forms of credit provision as the key assistance mechanism. In most cases also the programmes examined have a religious affiliation, frequently Christian, but none discriminate in implementing their programme between Christians and non-Christians. In almost all cases examined or reviewed in this study, the indigenous CIGP programme has at least one foreign partner. In some instances the indigenous CIGP came into being in response to the offer of financial, material, technical and spiritual support from the overseas NGO partner.

The success of the programmes is measured in material terms, that is, increased employment and family income — resulting in improved nutrition, education, and wealth — plus cost-effective and sustainable delivery of aid. In so doing the underlying thesis of the book relies on the assumption that the abolition of chronic hunger, a decline in unfulfilled basic needs, and improved employment and income-earning prospects at the household level are desirable outcomes. That is, they are positively correlated with improvement in the quality of life — in human welfare, personal dignity and self-worth — of the intended beneficiaries.

By these criteria, the study seeks to assess the development experience of the poor households that are the client group of NGOs. It also uses these criteria to investigate why they have succeeded where others have done little more than till the barren soil. The aim is to present their experiences, their stratagems, their arguments and the supporting facts in a way that can enable others to emulate and expand on the success that has been theirs alone for too long.

The brief drawn from the Oxford Conference stressed the need to target the study's attention on how committed organizations can make a difference in the battle against systemic poverty in the Third World. While it is true that valuable lessons can be learned from failed projects (we did come across a few of these on our travels), time and resource constraints forced us to concentrate on projects with a reputation for success. In so doing the project sought out examples that appear to offer the opportunity for replication and emulation, plus access to appropriate documentation that interested readers are free to follow up at their leisure. The nature of the successes we have sought to document involves several measures of 'programme impact' on sustained income and employment flows. By so doing there is no implication intended concerning alternative measures of success. Our field visits did bring to light some of these alternatives, especially those typically associated with community building, capacity for self-reliance and personal expressions of pride and satisfaction with what was being achieved. These are more subjective as indicators of success than those that this study has sought to utilize. Nonetheless, it bears saying that successful credit-based income-generation projects share a commitment to community building and to boosting the personal dignity and self-perception of all those involved, not least the borrower and the beneficiaries of the investments for which loans provided finance.

Philosophically, the author shared a consensus with the Project Steering Committee on the unacceptable opportunity cost of allocating my research time, resources and emotional energy to the study of projects judged by others as failures. These are likely to indicate things to avoid, but they are also likely to teach more about 'how to fail' than 'how to succeed'. Research for this book has, therefore, concentrated field work on visits with projects with a reputation for success. Overall, however, it is my impression that the conventional notion of success does not sit easily in this context if left unqualified. Once one gets behind the statistics and the published record, one soon finds that the success of the projects visited can be traced to the fact that:

○ they have a reputation for having fewer problems
○ they seem to have made fewer mistakes; and
○ they could point to or document desired consequences of their activities more readily than others.

Consequently, the objective criteria of success which the study seeks to emphasize must be viewed in broader terms than the purely financial or quantifiable. This has involved coming to grips with processes described in the literature by terms such as 'empowerment', 'conscientization', and 'change-agents', the current buzz-words in community development circles. I am yet to be convinced that these are a useful addition to the professional jargon. If they convey a sense that successful CIGPs encourage local self-reliance, reward self-help, maximize indigenous management and promote a commitment to 'participant ownership' of the programme then I, for one, have no quarrel with these terms, for these are the elements of which success is made.

The reader should not look to this study for a recipe of how to succeed in the implementation of credit-based income-generation programmes for the poor. The ingredients of success are to be found in appropriate responses to the circumstances in which a programme is to be implemented. To be sure, there are some general guidelines that can be set down and defended, and the study has attempted to identify and present these, but the nuts and bolts of daily administration (for example, whether loan repayments should be daily, weekly or some other period by country or culture) do not lend themselves to prescriptive treatment from afar.

Acknowledgements

THIS BOOK IS based on one attempt to document the experiences of others in the design and conduct of income- and employment-generation projects in the Third World. It has benefited from the generosity of many individuals and groups, too many to name separately here. (A list of programmes visited and an extensive bibliography are appended.)

The book draws freely from the life experiences of programme beneficiaries as well as committed individuals who have devoted their efforts to collaboration with the poor as programme and project sponsors, leaders, administrators and, most of all, partners. Field research involved lengthy discussions with project beneficiaries and personnel during visits to income-generation programmes in Indonesia, Philippines, Bangladesh, India, Sri Lanka, Kenya and Zimbabwe. Our aim was to restrict our visits to programmes that had a reputation for success. In the main, what we found amply demonstrated why the programmes we were privileged to visit had gained this reputation.

I trust that this document conveys not only the lessons and common characteristics of successful programmes but also the genuine enthusiasm with which the programme staff toil with the poor. There is an excitement that comes of doing something worthwhile and that clearly works. The projects we visited reflected this in various degrees and confirmed the depth of development potential yet to be had from replication and further support for similar programmes, wherever there are 'communities of the poor'.

In addition to an extensive programme of field visits, I also had the advantage of support and wisdom from an active Income-Generation Project Steering Committee, chaired by K.W. (Bill) Taylor. His experience as a former senior official, of almost 25 years standing, with the United Nations

Development Programme (UNDP), a successful business-man in his own right and the founder of the Foundation for Development Co-operation, was a most valued resource, that he allowed me to mine unselfishly. I am particularly grateful for the constructive criticism to which he subjected each draft of the study. The Project Steering Committee was central in identifying projects to visit. Their combined experience and familiarity with this field of development made my task that much easier. I commend the Steering Committee for their assistance and believe that the results vindicate the decisions taken.

During the course of field-work and research I benefited greatly from the opportunity to present ideas and preliminary results at a number of seminars and informal discussion groups. In particular I acknowledge those who organized and participated in meetings at World Vision International, Los Angeles; the World Bank and US AID in Washington DC; the Ford Foundation, New York and Nairobi offices; the Zadok Australia economists' group; the Sydney Christian Economists' group, the 'global partnership' conference, Canberra (sponsored by World Vision Australia); the Oxford Conference; and a number of academic seminars at universities in Australia and Britain. The final draft also reflects the comments of a large number of persons who read early versions and were kind enough to send me their comments in writing. All errors and omissions that remain are the responsibility of the author.

Most able, sensitive and efficient logistical support was provided by David Bussau, Secretary to the Project Steering Committee, and colleagues at Maranatha Trust, Sydney. They and their many friends in projects around the world gave generously to ensure that field trips were both productive and memorable experiences. The caring hospitality unreservedly extended while I was in the field served to underline the fundamental and shared view of all project workers whom we were able to visit: that at the centre of the development process must be the protection and promotion of human dignity.

Thanks must also go to Deakin Foundation and the Centre for Applied Social Research, Deakin University, which hosted the study and provided the means by which donor support for the project could be administered. Grateful acknowledgement is given to Mr K. W. Taylor for his financial support to the Deakin Foundation for the project. In addition I am most indebted to Evangelisches Missionswerk (EMW), Maranatha Trust, Opportunity International, and World Vision International for their support, both budgetary and otherwise. Assistance received from the Foundation for Development Co-operation towards the publication of this research is gratefully acknowledged.

Lastly but not least I thank my family for their unreserved support and encouragement, especially during my lengthy absences for field-work. Only those who have survived the pressures of single parenting when there are three under six at home can know the deep debt I owe my wife, Kate.

Joe Remenyi
Deakin University
July 1990

Mat weaving: an important domestic skill that generates cash and employment

Preparing the days' output for sale. Guatemala

1: The importance of being poor

FOR ONE FIFTH of humanity, i.e., a billion people world-wide, the daily reality is abject and chronic poverty. It is not a poverty that they choose or one that they can readily escape, without help. It is a poverty that we cannot ignore for it is, in the main, 'systematic poverty' which is the outcome of our own indifference as well as the economic and political processes of which we are all a part.

The unrequited states of poverty and deprivation are the outcomes of the processes that have rendered widespread poverty in the Third World to 'chronic' status. These processes have become institutionalized and are now both pervasive and pernicious. The systemic poverty that is the result of these processes falls most heavily on those described in this book as the 'hidden poor' — women, children, the frail and the old. But the processes that keep people poor are also reversible. What is needed is the will to do what is necessary and the openness to learn from those in the world who have gained from practical experience the wisdom that can make the difference for many in poverty.

In his influential book, *Comfortable Compassion* (1987), Charles Elliott writes:

> the Ethiopian crisis . . . seemed soluble in the sense that . . . people could be prevented from dying . . . overcoming the poverty of 800 million people on three continents does not seem a soluble problem in any equivalent sense. (p. 12)

This telling comment underlines one of the fundamental reasons why the immediate alleviation of systemic poverty has not been a criterion widely applied in the choice of development priorities, or in the evaluation of development projects and progammes. The alleviation of systemic poverty is a difficult criterion to accept as one's task-master. It is much easier to respond to a current emergency, or to join the ever

1

popular 'modernization' bandwagon that is the bread and butter of professional development planners, government agencies and expatriate experts. (For a disturbing but important account of how even the best efforts of official development and can go sorely wrong, see Hancock, 1989. A more sympathetic view can be found in Cassen, 1986.)

Professional development experts are especially well versed in the identification and design of expensive and large-scale 'projects of national significance'. Not only do these larger projects 'move a lot of money quickly', but they are prepared with an eye to the level of statistical detail, documentation and accountability procedures needed by multilateral and bilateral donor development assistance agencies. One should commend the commitment to accountability and documentation sought in these projects. One should not, however, naively accept the veracity of the data on which they are based or the assumption that, being of national significance, the benefits realized will flow to the bulk of the population. The potential benefits that projects of national significance are said to promise are typically described as percolating throughout the economy, to the improved economic welfare of all members and sections of society. Indeed, if one examines the bulk of major development projects supported by donor agencies, both public and private, one will find claims of this sort. It is not unusual for the project documentation to be replete with official estimates of the number of persons/households expected to benefit in the immediate and medium term. Despite these estimates and the best intentions of development planners, however, the outcome for the poor has, at best, not been encouraging. The successes of the 'green revolution' in tropical agriculture notwithstanding and the fact that we can all point to one or more apparently successful examples in the global development record, the number of desperately poor people in the Third World is increasing and not declining. It is difficult, therefore, to reject the conclusion that the benefits of development in the Third World have largely by-passed the poor. The benefits that do trickle down are too little too late. Development (read 'alleviation of systemic poverty') through modernizing influences of projects of national significance in the Third World is the soft option that has failed, yet it continues to dominate development planning and official development assistance, as it has since the second world war.

2

The poor in developing countries not only remain with us, but their numbers are annually swelled by the millions. If development is succeeding, it is only in the limited sense that certain sectors of Third World economies are being modernized. The modernization process has not, alas, led to a decline in the numbers of persons for whom abject poverty is a daily struggle throughout most of the Third World. For humanity at large, and more especially those with a deep religious commitment to the poor, this fact must be unacceptable, if not intolerable.

Who are the poor?

Although this study is about income-generation projects, it is also about people; in particular the people who are the intended beneficiaries of such projects. It is the poor on whom those who implement these successful CIGPs must rely as partners if their efforts are to have a sustained impact. However, before we can meaningfully discuss this process of 'working with the poor', it is critical that we are agreed on: 'who are the poor, where are they to be found, and what the poor do to survive'. At first thought these questions may seem obvious, even trite. But when we attempt to become specific we soon find that there is more here of importance than at first meets the eye.

The poor are not concentrated in either the city or in the country, though the proportion of the population that is in poverty tends to be greater in the rural districts. The 'systemic poor', however, are typically landless, living in a money economy, and lacking in sources of bargaining power necessary to rid themselves of their place in the 'poverty economy'. At its most general, to be economically poor in the Third World means that one belongs to a household which has access to income that is well below the national average, whether one is landless or not. In this study the income standard below which one is regarded as poor is defined as, 'persons coming from households with a total household annual cash income less than one half the national average'. On the basis of this definition, the World Bank's statistics on income distribution by household define as poor not less than one half of the households of developing countries. The 'poorest of the poor', those referred to already as the one-fifth of humanity living in abject and chronic

3

poverty, are merely a sub-set of a much larger world of poverty. Consider the statistics on income distributions in selected selected countries shown in Table 1.1.

The primary conclusion on poverty that can be drawn from the statistics in Table 1.1 is frightening but inescapable: to be genuinely poor is the norm in most developing countries. Acknowledgement of this fact is a critical step if we are determined to reform received wisdom and target development to benefit first and foremost the poor.

Income distribution by household is not the same as wealth distribution by household, but it is generally true that the wealthiest households also have the highest incomes. The reverse is also true — the poorest households have the lowest income earnings. Similarly, per capita GDP is not the same as average household income. Nonetheless, from the data in Table 1.1 we can get a feel for the extent of poverty by comparing the distribution of household income to the top 20 per cent of income-earning households with that going to households at the bottom of the pecking order. We can say with some confidence that households in the bottom three quintiles, i.e. the bottom 60 per cent, meet easily the poverty definition given above. National data, such as the latest official statistics (1985) of the National Economic Development Authority (NEDA) in the Philippines, are consistent with these results. NEDA identifies the incidence of poverty in the rural sector at 63.2 per cent and in the urban sector at 52 per cent for the Philippines as a whole. My discussions in the field suggest that a similar correspondence holds in other developing countries.

In relative terms the figures on income distribution across households indicate that poverty is least stark but most prevalent in Asia. Here the top 20 per cent receive almost nine times the share of total annual household income of the bottom 20 per cent. In Africa they receive more than sixteen times as much, and in Latin Americ they receive in excess of twenty times. The second and third quintiles from the bottom do not fare all that much better, so taken together the bottom 60 per cent of households in each of Asia, Africa and Latin America receive less in total annual income, by a very wide margin, than the 20 per cent of top income-earning households. However, the primary locus of world poverty remains in Asia for it is here that the absolute size of populations is so massive.

4

Table 1.1 Income distribution in selected countries

Country	Year	% of household income going to					GNP per head US$, 1985
		lowest 20%	2nd 20%	3rd 20%	4th 20%	highest 20%	
Asia							
Bangladesh	1981–2	6.6	10.7	15.3	22.1	45.3	150
India	1975–6	7.0	9.2	13.9	20.5	49.4	270
Sri Lanka	1980–1	5.8	10.1	14.1	20.3	49.8	380
Indonesia	1976	6.6	7.8	12.6	23.6	49.6	530
Philippines	1985	5.2	8.9	13.2	20.2	52.5	580
Thailand	1975–6	5.6	9.6	13.9	21.1	49.8	800
Malaysia	1973	3.5	7.7	12.4	20.3	56.1	2000
S. Korea	1976	5.7	11.2	15.4	22.4	45.3	2150
Hong Kong	1980	5.4	10.8	15.2	21.6	47.0	6230
Simple average		5.7	9.5	14.0	21.3	49.4	1455
Africa							
Kenya	1976	2.6	6.3	11.5	19.2	60.4	290
Zambia	1976	3.4	7.4	11.2	16.9	61.1	390
Egypt	1974	5.8	10.7	14.7	20.8	48.0	610
Ivory Coast	1985–6	2.4	6.2	10.9	19.1	61.4	660
Mauritius	1980–1	4.0	7.5	11.0	17.0	60.5	1090
Simple average		3.6	7.6	11.9	18.6	58.3	6100

Table 1.1 continued

Country	Year	% of household income going to					GNP per head US$, 1985
		lowest 20%	2nd 20%	3rd 20%	4th 20%	highest 20%	
L. America							
El Salvador	1976–7	5.5	10.0	14.8	22.4	47.3	820
Peru	1972	1.9	5.1	11.0	21.0	61.0	1010
Brazil	1972	2.0	5.0	9.4	17.0	66.6	1640
Mexico	1977	2.9	7.0	12.0	20.4	57.7	2080
Panama	1973	2.0	5.2	11.0	20.0	61.8	2100
Argentina	1970	4.4	9.7	14.1	21.5	50.3	2130
Venezuela	1970	3.0	7.3	12.9	22.8	54.0	3080
Simple average		2.8	7.0	12.2	20.7	57.0	1840
Donor countries							
Britain	1979	7.0	11.5	17.0	24.8	39.7	8870
Netherlands	1981	8.3	14.1	18.2	23.2	36.2	10,020
Australia	1975–6	5.4	10.0	15.0	22.5	47.1	11,920
W. Germany	1978	7.9	12.5	17.0	23.1	39.5	12,080
Japan	1979	8.7	13.2	17.5	23.1	37.5	12,840
Canada	1981	5.3	11.8	18.0	24.9	40.0	14,120
Norway	1982	6.0	12.9	18.3	24.6	38.2	15,400
USA	1980	5.3	11.9	17.9	25.0	39.9	17,480
Simple average		6.7	12.2	17.4	20.8	39.8	12,840

Source: World Bank, *World Development Report*, various years.

The 60 per cent of households at the bottom of the income distribution receive an annual income that is well below the poverty standard of household income. There is considerable justification for choosing this level of income as the cut-off below which one is defined as 'poor'. It is a poverty line that has intuitive appeal and forces us to consider seriously how households survive at these meagre levels of cash income. The fact that this standard means that when we speak of the 'community of the poor' we refer to at least one-half and often three-quarters of the households in some of the least developed countries is not a result from which we should resile. This number is an objective result of the application of an eminently defensible objective criterion. It should serve to underline the importance of raising the alleviation of systemic poverty in the list of priorities sought in development planning and development assistance.

The implication of these data is that there are many many more poor people in the Third World than is indicated by the 'poorest of the poor' scenarios published by the World Bank and United Nations agencies. The population of the poorest of the poor that these agencies quote refer to the 'chronically poor' only. Table 1.1 gives us a view into the full extent of the whole 'community of the poor' in developing countries. The fact that the size of the global poverty problem is two or three times the size of that associated with the 'poorest of the poor' is not a comment on the statistics or the definition of poverty employed here. It is an indictment of the unequal distribution of the benefits of economic progress that developing countries have achieved in the past generation and more.

No matter how we might be horrified at the result, it would require an enormous margin of error for us to reject the conclusion that 'poverty is not a problem of the few in the tropics, it is the normal condition of the bulk of people'. The one billion or so persons that the World Bank describes as the 'chronically poor' are, therefore, no more than a slice of a far larger group. Alas, if we see or are shown 'the poor' on television or in the print media, it is largely this slice, the poorest of the poor, that we see. Their equally important and worthy neighbours in the community of the poor are just as real and just as invisible as the silent majority are quiet and unheard in more comfortable economies.

What does it mean to be poor?

If we are to know our client groups, the poor and microenterprise entrepreneurs in poverty, we must look beyond the popular image of poverty as some sort of homogeneous mass of unfortunates. There is almost as much diversity among the poor as there is in society as a whole. Once we grasp the significance of this for the design and implementation of poverty-alleviation programmes, CIGPs in particular, we also find it useful and of considerable heuristic value to consider the poor as made up of distinct sub-groups defined by the level of enterprise or type of economic survival activity each pursues. For our purposes there are five such sub-groups or 'levels of poverty' that seem to offer productive insights. Consider the Pyramid of Poverty schema presented in Figure 1.1.

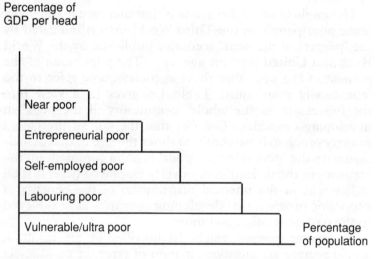

Figure 1.1 *The poverty pyramid in the Third World*

At the very bottom of the Poverty Pyramid are those who Michael Lipton (1988) described as the ultra poor but whom we could also describe as the vulnerable poor. This sub-group is dominated by women and children who, together with the frail and the old, are essentially dependent upon the earnings of others for their survival, despite the economic contribution they make to the survival activities of poor households. There is reason to believe that the vulnerable/

ultra poor make up the largest sub-group in the community of the poor. This remains a hypothesis to be tested, however, and it may well prove to be the next strata of persons in poverty, the labouring poor group, which also includes men, women and children, that is in the majority.

Second at the base of the Poverty Pyramid are the labouring poor. This sub-group consists of both self-employed persons and itinerant employees. The greater number of the sub-group relies heavily on the sale of their labour as unskilled workers on a daily basis for cash and other income in kind. A significant number find self-employment in the various scavenging trades, selling their finds on a daily basis for cash income. No one in the labouring poor group receives or can count upon stable full-time employment; they must all be regarded as underemployed. In developing countries the labouring poor are ubiquitous on building sites, around infrastructure construction works, on farms as agricultural labourers, and in piece-work employment. Child labour and domestic service are also included in this sub-group wherever the combined household income earned is less than the national average.

Many of the vulnerable/ultra poor are dependent on the fortunes of these opportunist hawkers of labour for their livelihood and survival. Males tend to outnumber females in the sub-group but this is not universally true. In the absence of specific numbers, logic and observation during field-research suggests that the labouring poor is the second largest group among the poor. Because the labouring poor includes many women and children, some commentators on earlier drafts of this text have argued that they form the largest group in the Poverty Pyramid. Since the number of women and children who earn their survival in this way on a full-time basis is limited, however, I adhere to my hypothesis that the labouring poor are the second largest sub-group.

The next sub-group is made up of those we describe as the self-employed poor. Their number is dominated by persons who basically work on their own account, but many also employ up to five persons, not necessarily all full time. The enterprises in which they find a niche are ubiquitous, covering tailoring, furniture making and repair, store-keeping and mobile corner or side-street vending enterprises, the preparation of popular foods for sale on consignment that are the local equivalents of developed economies 'fast-foods' or the production of one or more of the many other necessaries of life that the poor 'buy' on a regular, often daily basis.

The self-employed poor are the backbone of the micro-enterprise sector in developing countries. Women are often in the majority in the sub-group. The enterprises run by the self-employed offer a commercial outlet for talents learnt in the home environment, and form an important source of survival employment, often part-time employment, for members of the vulnerable/ultra poor, especially children and the frail.

A most important and dynamic sub-group in the Poverty Pyramid is the cadre of entrepreneurial poor who are also self-employed but run enterprises employing more than five persons. Despite their success as small-business operators and employers, a significant number of the entrepreneurial poor remain below the poverty line as defined on page 3. The entrepreneurial poor are no longer as poor as their employees or those who belong to lower levels in the Poverty Pyramid, but they remain enmeshed in enterprises that employ the poor, are located in poor districts and typically produce an output destined for sale to consumers who are themselves chronically poor. Shoemaking and repairs, cosmetics manufacture, various textile trades, metal fabrication firms, small plastic and polymer-based production factories are examples of trades in which the entrepreneurial poor can be found. Despite the risks associated with their business investments that this sub-group takes, the net income the entrepreneurial poor receive from the profits they generate all too often does not exceed the poverty level.

The least materially deprived sub-group in the Poverty Pyramid is the near poor. These persons belong to households whose livelihood is intimately linked to the economic activity of the poor but they typically enjoy an annual household income that is in excess of the poverty level as we have defined it. However, for a great number of the near poor annual earnings per head remain well below the national average.

A majority are substantial employers of poorer people but many also find themselves beyond the poverty threshold because they and other household members are fortunate enough to have found regular employment as a guard, gardener, driver, cleaner, human services provider or basic administrative person, often with the government, the military or the local arm of a foreign enterprise. Total earnings are, however, not enough to bring the household into the socio-economic middle class. The near poor continue to live in the poorer neighbourhoods, consume wage goods produced by the poor for the poor and lack a sufficient asset base to have access to the lending facilities of the formal banking sector.

In one way or another all persons in the Poverty Pyramid have benefited from the CIGPs examined in the course of this study. The direct beneficiaries, however, come mainly from the levels of poverty to which the majority of the loans are made, that is, the self-employed, entrepreneurial and near poor. In so far as the borrowers use their loans to generate employment or additional income, indirect benefits flow to members of the labouring and the vulnerable poor. The welfare-linked CIGPs also stress non-credit socio-economic activities that enable individuals to progress more easily from a lower to a higher level of the Poverty Pyramid. For example, in Bangladesh the CIGPs run by the Christian Commission for Development (CCDB), the Bangladesh Rural Advancement Committee (BRAC) and the Grameen Bank programmes specialize in helping members of the vulnerable and labouring poor to become self-employed. In contrast with the frustrating experience the poor have had with the essentially ineffective trickle-down effects of many macro-economic development projects of national significance, the CIGPs of these NGOs have immediate and obvious benefits. These programmes work directly with the poor, fostering growth in productivity and value added in enterprises that employ the poor and produce 'wage-goods' for consumption by the poor.

One could be excused, therefore, for suggesting that to ask, 'Who are the poor?', is not too simple a question. Would that it were! It is not enough to know that the poor are those with too little money. Such a statement gives us none of the insight and capacity to empathize with the poor that flows naturally from the simple classification presented in the Poverty Pyramid. Yet it is the neglect of even the simple facts contained in such a classification that has allowed the belief that 'We know who the poor are' to relegate poor women and children to the status of invisible poor of the Third World.

It is not far from the truth to say that when one speaks of poverty in the Third World one is speaking of women and

11

children. Their invisibility to development planners and development professionals generally goes a long way to explain why development projects aimed at the direct and immediate alleviation of systemic poverty have not played a greater role in Third World economic development than they have or ought to have done.

In summary, what can we say that is of general importance but too often neglected in development planning and the development project cycle, about the poor of the developing world?

○ There is enormous heterogeneity in and between each level of the Poverty Pyramid.
○ Typically the systemic poor are not active members of the highly visible, formal, private or public sectors in developing countries. Neither are they the beneficiaries of government welfare largesse or public-sector employees. The poor can be found in the private-enterprise dominated 'poor economy', often referred to as the informal sector at the edge of the modern monetized economy, in both the rural and the urban sectors in developing countries. It is here where tens of thousands of individual enterprises compete to provide basic survival needs, that is, wage-goods such as food, clothing, health services, basic training (often on the job in an informal apprenticeship mode), shelter, and 'rudimentary luxuries such as alcohol, soft drinks, flowers, cosmetics, in exchange for the earnings from lowly paid 'unskilled labour'.
○ The poor are those whose capacity to generate 'value added' is very limited and often constrained by the socio-economic processes that work to keep the poor poor. Critical amongst these processes is the denial of access to the essential resources that the poor need to improve their productivity and capacity to be self-reliant. Investment finance is one of these key resources.
○ The poor are indeed those with the least income. In the course of the field-work for this project household income levels and wage rates were examined as closely as possible. It seems safe to say in consequence that as a rule of thumb poor households often earn, on an annualized basis not only less than the national average, but on a household basis, less than half the published GNP per head for the country in question.

12

o The poor account for the bulk of households in developing countries. Hence, to work towards a development strategy that is of direct benefit to the poor is consistent with doing the greatest good not only to the most needy but also the greatest number.

o Flexibility is one of the more important keys to survival in the world of the poor. Consequently, the poor, no matter from which level of the Poverty Pyramid they might hail, are often multiple-job holders, moving by the season, the time of the week or the time of day between occupations. In many senses the poor are the true 'permanent part-timers' in the workforce of the Third World, choosing this mobile lifestyle in order to minimize risk and maximize capacity to take advantage of changes, possibly very sudden changes, in market conditions and opportunities.

o The bulk of the population and, therefore, the greatest number of poor people in the Third World are in the rural districts. Despite this, there is reason to believe that concentration of CIGP effort on the creation of non-farm employment opportunities will have a bigger impact on the alleviation of systemic poverty than investments that augment agricultural employment. This does not mean that agricultural development should be neglected, rather it acknowledges that the pace of urbanization, including 'rural urbanization', and the need to raise productivity in agriculture by reducing underemployment in that sector presents a *prima facie* case for concentrating employment generation in non-farm and off-farm employment opportunities. Such employment creation in the rural sector of Third World countries is critical if the number of job opportunities is to increase in pace with numbers entering the workforce from the rural population.

Poverty and development: the macroeconomic bias

A number of implications for development planning suggest themselves. Systemic poverty is not only a global problem that traditional approaches to development have not succeeded in reducing but, after four decades of development effort, the poor still represent not less than the lowest 40 per cent of households and possibly as many as two-thirds of all households. In Asia, at least three-fifths of households are in the bottom 30 per cent of the income distribution. In Africa

13

the comparable figures are three-fifths and the bottom quarter, while in the Latin Americas three-fifth of households are in the bottom 20 per cent of the income distribution. Clearly, poverty is where the bulk of the people are and development cannot be deemed to have succeeded unless it has a significant positive impact on the lot of the most popular sector in all developing countries, the poverty sector.

Distribution issues are central to development policy and especially so when we are concerned with how best to help the poor. It does not follow though that an achievable goal of poverty alleviation could be to raise 100 per cent of the poor from the bottom 20 per cent of the income distribution to the top 20 per cent. A more realistic goal is to reduce the absolute numbers on low, poverty-level incomes. This may involve some redistribution from the rich to the poor through government welfare programmes and the like. But a more sustainable development strategy, one that eschews the handout mentality, is preferable. The oft-repeated adage is apposite — if you give a poor person a fish, there is a meal today; if you enable a poor person to become a fisherman, the means are there for meals to be furnished every day. The change to a self-help strategy of development from the traditional 'macroeconomic modernization' approach is not easy.

The founder and long time head of the Indian Statistical Institute, P. C. Mahalanobis (1963), member of the influential Indian Planning Commission and architect of the Indian development plans that replaced the Gandhi-inspired 'small is beautiful' approach to development of the 1950s, believed that development demanded a period of austerity and suffering for the typical Indian household. The Indian development strategy in the 1960s was imbued with the notion that if the country was to become a member of the powerful developed nations, it must develop the capacity to 'build the machines that build the machines'. The Government of India Planning Commission put it this way in its preliminary justification of the provisions and privations proposed in the second Indian five-year plan:

Rapid industrialization and diversification of the economy is thus the core of development. But if industrialization is to be rapid enough, the country must aim at developing basic industries and industries which make machines to make machines needed for further development. (Indian Planning Commission, 1956:21)

14

The capital investment required for industrialization (read modernization) would demand the diversion of massive amounts of current production from consumption to investment purposes. The cost would be a decline in the consumption standards of the average Indian household. This result, claimed Mahalanobis, is unavoidable if sustained development is to be achieved in the long term (see Mahalanobis, 1963:29 and 48f; and Rao *et al.*:23). The fact that this period of deprivation may last for at least a generation did not deter Mahalanobis and his colleagues on the Indian Planning Commission from embracing, with enthusiasm, this 'industrial modernization first' strategy of development. Nor did it deter development planners in many other developing countries — in the 1960s and 1970s 'modernization first' five-year development plans were all the rage; no self-respecting developing country would be without one.

In the main, the five-year development plans of most developing countries through the 1960s and 1970s followed India's lead in the choice of development priorities. Industrial investment and modernization were favoured over projects of income and employment generation for the immediate alleviation of poverty. It was accepted openly that such a strategy of development is likely to see, at least in the short term, an increase in poverty. But given time poverty alleviation was confidently expected to be a by-product of the economic growth flowing from modernization. This process has since been characterized as the trickle-down theory of development.

The legacy of this development path has been not only an increase in deprivation generally and growth in the numbers of households in poverty in the tropics but also a commitment in the Third World to development strategies that favour modernization over poverty alleviation as an immediate goal of official planning. Some readers may find this a long bow to draw, given the poverty-oriented rhetoric that inevitably accompanies the announcement of every new development project of national significance financed by the World Bank, a major bilateral donor, or some other development assistance agency. Be it an infrastructure project, such as a new dam, power plant, highway, airport, upgraded port facility or new industrial development project. Every World Bank or United Nations final project appraisal document, and most bilateral official development assistance (ODA)

15

project documents, bristle with numbers that purport to identify the many thousands of ordinary people who are expected to benefit from each new project funded. I have no quarrel with the rhetoric, only with the reality. If the rhetoric is real, why are there still so many poor households/persons in the Third World? If all those World Bank, United Nations and bilateral ODA development projects of national significance really do have the thousands of beneficiaries identified in their project announcements, why is it that there are still so many people waiting desperately for their share? Something has gone seriously amiss.

The reality is that successful development in the Third World has largely been for the few and bypassed the poor. There has not been a broadbased distribution of the benefits of the substantial developments that have occurred in the Third World. The trickle-down approach has not worked. It may work in the long term, but many citizens of the Third World will by then be dead. Moreover, the benefits of this trickle-down, 'development through modernization' approach to economic progress will continue to bypass the poor so long as development projects ignore the obstacles that prevent the poor from meeting their immediate basic need to overcome hunger, homelessness, illiteracy and the denial of access to modern-sector services and resources. One grossly neglected basic need is access to the financial resources the poor need to invest in their own betterment.

The professional language used to describe poverty and the development process all too often creates a mindset that unconsciously biases development planning against the interests of the poor: poverty is something to be got rid of, banished; the corollary — getting rid of poverty means getting rid of the poor through better macroeconomic policies and plans. This attitude typically does not lead development planners to choose projects that involve working with the poor. A people-oriented strategy is passed over in favour of more bricks and mortar 'for the people'. Is it any wonder that virtually every major city in the Third World has had its slum clearance project that managed to push the poor 'out of sight, out of mind'. Slum clearance may beautify the cities of the Third World, but it has brought little joy to the poor that have been displaced.

CIGPs offer an alternative strategy for getting rid of poverty; one that involves setting in place procedures and oppor-

16

tunities that enable the poor to 'help themselves' rise above poverty and join the ranks of the well-to-do. Before this can happen, a revolution is needed; a revolution that rejects the traditional approach to development as largely irrelevant to those who must survive at the poverty end of the economic spectrum in developing countries. Urban renewal, slum regularization, land reform and modern-sector industrial development have not delivered to the poor of the Third World the escape from poverty that these essentially government controlled programmes have promised. In too many cases the contrary has happened, pushing the poor further into the margins of urban slums, isolating their opportunities for economic advancement to the often illegal informal sector at the edge of society and the money economy. Here they must contend with restricted access to resources and the operation of rules and regulations that act as unseen but virulent barriers to escape from poverty.

The apparent inability of the poor to benefit significantly from large development projects that are sector-wide, regional in focus or concerned with industrial modernization has prompted a rethink of how this situation can be remedied, especially on the part of private-sector development enterprises and development-oriented NGOs. Different groups have found different solutions, but in each case there are common characteristics. The most consistent finding is the need to eschew the destructive power of patronage and well-intentioned charitable hand-outs. What is essential both for success and the promotion of true human development is the need for donor organizations to trust the poor whom they seek to assist, and to do so by being prepared to 'work with the poor' as opposed to 'for the poor'. The distinction is subtle but fundamental.

In the foregoing the traditional approach to poverty alleviation (i.e., poverty alleviation through development) has been severely criticized. It would not do, however, if the impression was left that the writer does not acknowledge the achievements that have resulted from the activities of the World Bank, development agencies, or government development programmes. The contrary is true, and in another place I have written about some of these achievements as they relate to agriculture and the green revolution; (see, for example, Remenyi, 1990, 1988 & 1986; and Coxhead and Remenyi, 1985).

Income-generation projects and community development

Virtually every CIGP programme encountered in the course of this study bespeaks a commitment to community development goals in addition to the alleviation of systemic poverty and growth in the microenterprise sector. For those familiar with the credit programme and community development disasters of the 1950s and 1960s, the community development focus associated with the CIGP route to poverty alleviation seems tainted with an air of *déjà-vu* that is cause for nervousness, if not scepticism about the prospects of CIGPs as a new phenomenon in development. Are CIGPs merely a discredited idea in new clothing?

In order to answer this question it is critical that we come to understand what it is that the practitioners of CIGPs do today that sets them apart from the community development workers of the 1950s and 1960s. If we are of a mind to believe the rhetoric, the answer to this question can be found in the concept of empowerment. The catch cry of today's community development workers is that 'community development without empowerment is no development at all'. Today's practitioners also claim that community development failed thirty years ago because the development professionals of that time didn't realize the importance of empowerment. Is there any substance behind these claims? If there is, why should we expect that CIGPs as a strategy of community development will fare any better? To deduce satisfactory answers, we must dig a little deeper.

We begin by contrasting what was claimed to be the essence of community development in the 1950s and 1960s with what is meant by empowerment in the contemporary community development literature. Holdcroft (1984) writes as follows of the 1950s and 60s:

> Community development was defined as a process, method, programme, institution, and/or movement which (a) involves people on a community basis in the solution of their common problems, (b) teaches and insists upon the use of democratic processes in the joint solution of community problems, and (c) activates and/or facilitates the transfer of technology to the people of a community for more effective solution of their common problems. Join efforts to solve common problems democratically and scientifically on a community basis were seen as the essential elements of CD. (p. 47)

Now consider the following definition of empowerment taken from a recent overview of a major symposium on the role of NGOs in development. Drabek (1988) describes empowerment as: 'enabling the poor to take control of the decision making processes which affect their lives . . .' (p. 10).

Is there a difference? The final sentences in the quotes from Holdcraft and Drabek certainly sound similar. There is, however, an important difference between the two. The key departure is that today's CIGPs not only contribute to income and employment generation but the means employed to give the poor control of their lives is quite different. The most successful income- and employment-generation programmes consciously eschew paternalism by putting their faith in the poor as a cornerstone of the design and implementation of the CIGP. Consequently, as a matter of deliberate policy, CIGPs loosen the finance constraint in order that the poor may take charge of their own lives, provide themselves with the opportunity to be self-reliant and nurture grassroots structures that encourage individual initiative above charity or corporate dependence.

People-centred community development has a bad name in official development assistance circles because the attempt at grassroots community development a generation ago failed so tragically, not only because so little was achieved to help the poor or to accelerate village-level economic growth but also because a generation of development planners in the Third World were disillusioned against community-based strategies. Consequently, forced-paced, command-economy style, centrally-controlled development planning became the preferred path to modernization. New technology, government-run enterprises and infrastructure investments became the means by which less developed economies were to be dragged from backward poverty into prosperous modernity. Development for the people lost out in favour of growth in average GNP per head, increased domestic savings rates to finance the pursuit of modernity, population control and real economic benefits for future generations. These goals became the gods to which most development professionals, inside and outside the Third World, prayed.

The demise of community development a generation ago was tragic too because, in many respects, the wrong lesson was drawn. This claimed that development could not be accelerated without the imposition of long periods of economic hardship to ensure adequate levels of saving, investment and adoption of new technology. The importance of government as an actor in the development process was elevated beyond anything seen in peacetime in the free-market economies since the era of the mercantilists two centuries before. Private enterprise, individual initiative and the economist's fabled 'rational man' lost out to government-dictated priorities and five-year development plans.

It would be drawing too extreme a contrast to argue that the contemporary emphasis on empowerment as a strategy of community development differs because it requires the reinstatement of economic man or market-driven economic policies. Empowerment does, however, demand that the order of priorities in development return the individual to centre stage. At the policy and planning levels this means:

○ accurate targetting of the groups to be assisted (even where this involves confrontation with entrenched interests to remove injustices that prevent the poor from having access to human rights)
○ use of appropriate instruments of development assistance
○ involvement of the client group in decision making; and
○ the initiation of activities that do not exceed the capabilities of the people to sustain the projects of which they are meant to be the primary beneficiaries.

These requirements are not obviously inconsistent with the essential features of community development as it was conceived twenty and thirty years ago. Why didn't it work then? More important, why should we expect that empowerment will make all the difference and allow us to be confident that empowerment-linked community development founded on CIGPs will fare any better?

It would be wrong to trivialize the issues involved in answering this most difficult question by offering simple guidelines and unequivocal one-liners. However, with the benefit of hindsight, there are some considered observations that can be proffered:

○ The proponents of community development in the 1950s and 60s feared that unless development lifted the poor of the undeveloped world out of poverty, Third World peoples would join those who advocated revolution and enforced confiscation of wealth from the rich. Community

20

development seemed to offer a peaceful and democratic way in which everyone could win because the pie would be bigger and all would share the fruits of economic growth and new technology. History has shown that the benefits of development have not been shared equally despite the best efforts of the advocates of revolution and confiscation.

○ Post-Second World War economic planning in developing countries was based on misplaced confidence in the ability of government to compensate for market failures. Consequently, it was believed that free enterprise tempered by government-controlled Keynesian macroeconomics would ensure that where the private sector was unable to bring the benefits of development to the people, government deficit financing could be used to boost the flow of savings into modernization, government subsidies to investment could be used to overcome the disincentives of the poverty trap and social service programmes could be used to overcome the worst constraints of market failure for those in poverty. It is now history that the result has been a much more rapid growth of welfare than of private-sector output, a burgeoning in the role of the state in Third World economic activity and a distribution of the benefits of economic growth that consolidated the position of elites and the status quo of the poor as experts in the economics of survival.

○ Empowerment recognizes that it is folly to rely on one group to take decisions on behalf of another and expect them to eschew their own self-interest. The community development programmes of a generation past did exactly this by seeking to work through traditional village leaders, or those who already exhibited the trappings of modernization. Community development gave power over development resources and authority for the distribution of patronage to those who already had power — the literate and the non-poor. It was in their interests to support programmes that would see them, their families and friends the primary beneficiaries of development. As a result, the trickle-down of benefits to others was constrained to whatever was left after family and other obligations were met. Empowerment-linked community development through CIGPs is different in that they harness economic self-interest at an individual level and reject patronage or any

21

other form of dole-out as the foundation stone of a sustainable programme of development for the poor. Instead individual self-interest plus community and peer-group pressure are used to achieve economic discipline, such as meeting savings targets and repayment schedules, by the individual entrepreneur.

○ If we want to help the poor help themselves, we must know who the poor are, where to find them and how they seek their livelihood. The early attempts at grassroots community development, for example, worked through community leaders, very few of whom were representatives of the disadvantaged in society, especially the poor. Consequently, some very large groups found themselves disenfranchised, critically women and children. These two groups form the majority of those who populate the Poverty Pyramid and they are the main class of participants and beneficiaries in CIGPS.

The economics of survival

The economic activity of the poor is synonymous with the economics of survival. At the particular, microeconomic level the economics of survival cover the myriad of street vendors who serve meals to unskilled workers too poor to afford cooking facilities or storage capacity. There are also rickshaw drivers who transport goods and people to and from their slum or village compounds. In backyard repair shops and on street stalls families ply their untrained native skills to recycle materials recovered from rubbish bins and tips by the metal, glass, wood, plastic and rag pickers that are a ubiquitous feature of urban centres in developing countries. On the footpaths and in side-streets basic cobblering and clothing repair services are sold to passers-by. In village squares and urban street culverts simple wicker and bamboo baskets, floor mats and woven split bamboo walls for a rudimentary hut come from the nimble hands of folk no richer than those who purchase them. In rough-hewn work areas at the rear of the family home utilitarian furniture is produced from second-hand materials for use by local urban and rural poor. But most of all, there are the multitude of tiny street vendors and corner shops that supply staple foods and basic consumer goods (such as rice, flour, sugar, kerosene, LPG, cotton material, toiletries, usually on a daily basis, to poor households in the small quantities they can afford and effectively use with the minimum of waste.

The mosaic of activity in the poverty economy is not bland and uneventful. Its rich tapestry rings with the cry of traders haggling, the clash of hammers banging, the spark of ark-welders hissing and the clip of the tailors' scissors, just as it does in the modern formal economy, to which it abuts cheek by jowl and with which it interacts in various ways. The poverty economy is not isolated from the formal economy. It is merely starved of the life-blood that is essential to the prosperity of any monetized economy — liquidity. In the informal poverty economy a little money has to circulate rapidly to make up for the lack of liquidity of the poor. Households cannot afford to invest in stocks of food but buy in small quantities, as and when needed. Similarly, the entrepreneurial poor who manufacture goods for final consumption or on sub-contract to larger establishments cannot afford to build up stocks of materials when they are cheap because revenue from sales of current output is essential for the purchase of inputs for the next day's production.

The most important markets for the output of small and poor enterprises are the poor themselves. The millions of tiny enterprises that characterize the informal poverty economy provide goods at prices that the poor can afford. They provide these in quantities that are suitably small (for example, one egg, one cigarette) for effective use in the hands of consumers with little or no storage capacity. The commodities that the poor buy also exhibit a level of quality that foregoes the trappings of luxury, non-essential packaging and a margin for advertising. They are also offered to customers, especially in the case of food, fuel and water at times and in a manner suited to the often frenetic pace of life of those who must hustle and rush to exploit every opportunity to earn a few pence.

Risk-taking also has a uniquely onerous quality for the poor, a problem with which wealthier entrepreneurs do not normally have to contend. The poor are risk-averse because the consequences of failure, should a new technology, product or other innovation not succeed, go beyond the normal financial costs of bankruptcy. The loss of cash-flow can be disastrous not only to the survival of the business of a micro-entrepreneur in the informal poverty economy but to the survival of family and one's own body and soul as well.

Microentrepreneurs tend, therefore, to be very conservative in their investment decisions because they literally cannot afford to be wrong!

The scarcity of liquidity and investment capital among the poor is a critical reason why they remain poor. It is important, therefore, to examine the causes of the chronic cash-flow crisis that constrains their ability to help themselves.

Institutional perversities aside, about which we will have more to say later, it is difficult to ignore the low level of productivity of workers from poor communities and the high level of unemployment and underemployment as two significant contributing factors to the liquidity crisis that is the essence of being poor. The opportunity cost of labour measures the value of activities that could be undertaken other than that which currently commands attention. Hence, the opportunity cost of labour is low when its productivity is low. It is especially low when it is unemployed and not in demand. Anything that raises this opportunity cost, such as a fall in the level of unemployment, will relieve the cash-flow problem by increasing the opportunity to earn more income. A fall in unemployment increases the value of labour either because of an increase in demand or a rise in productivity. The result of either an increase in the demand for workers or a fall in the cost of production is a sustainable increase in the total amount paid in wages to workers drawn from the ranks of the poor. (A more formal presentation of why this is so is given in the Appendix: The Simple Economics of CIGP.)

What might cause such an increase in employment opportunities? Assume that the answer is the sudden availability of a new production technology that significantly reduces the cost of production through an increase in output per person employed per day. The increase in labour productivity that this change represents means that profit-motivated employers will want to hire additional workers up to the point where it is no longer profitable to employ any more. The demand for labour could rise for other reasons also. For example, in the above case we assumed that the profit margin increased because costs of production fell, price of the product remaining constant. Consider now that production conditions remain unchanged, but demand for the product being produced rises. It might rise because the product can now be sold in a market which was previously not open. An example might be the price rise that follows an increase in exports in response to a reduction in import tariffs levied by advanced economies on textiles or handicrafts exported from developing countries. In other words, the increase in demand means that more output can be sold at prices no lower than previously obtained in the smaller domestic market, if only additional supplies were available. In this situation it becomes profitable for employers to hire extra labour, even though physical output per worker has not increased. It is the 'value' of output per worker that has increased.

A successful CIGP can be expected to have either or even both of these effects, that is an increase in 'productivity' as well as an increase in value in response to a rise in demand. The impact of a successful CIGP can be described by an increase in the demand for labour at the going wage rate or an increase in total income. In summary, an income- and employment-generation project can work either through the finance of an improvement in the production process or through the demand side by increasing the demand for the products that are the output of labour's endeavours. Employment is derived from the demand for commodities and the aim is to either increase the efficiency of labour and thereby the profitability of employing more, or increase the value of the output of labour with a similar consequence for profits and the creation of job opportunities.

The reasons for the low level of productivity and high level of unemployment among the poor are legion. Not least among these is the lack of investment capacity by the poor. When survival expenditures command the bulk of what little cash income is received, little remains for investment purposes. It follows, therefore, that a potentially effective way in which to use income- and employment-generation initiatives to assist the poor is to bias the CIGP activities towards those investment opportunities that contribute to increases in the productivity and employment of the poor. A programme bias of this sort involves any one or a combination of relatively well understood economic processes, all of which amount to improving the value-added attributable to economic survival activities of the poor. These processes can be summarized thus:

○ a decline in unemployment and/or underemployment among the poor increases productivity by increasing average output per person

25

○ new technology, in the form of equipment or processes, can increase productivity by allowing output per person to rise without an increase in labour input or a fall in total value of output
○ introduction of new products can increase productivity by allowing economic resources to be shifted into more profitable lines of production
○ expansion into new markets increases productivity by enabling an increase in sales without having to reduce prices or cut profit margins
○ Readers interested in a more formal presentation and discussion of these processes are directed to the Appendix: The Simple Economics of CIGP.

The CIGPs that form the basis of this study have funded microenterprises that have contributed effectively to these processes.

Additive v competitive programmes

Development for the poor can and in some cases should involve 'taking from the rich to give to the poor', especially where socially undesirable monopolies and other unfair barriers to enterprise and initiative operate. Indeed, much of the opposition to programmes designed to help the poor help themselves comes from the entrenched interests whose fiefdoms are threatened by the competition that can follow the implementation of a CIGP by the poor. Traditional informal sector moneylenders may resent the loss of business and power that follows the loss of influence over former clients. Wealthy and middle-income consumers may oppose skills training for domestic servants for fear of losing affordable home help. In the majority of CIGPs observed for this study, direct confrontation with entrenched interests was not a problem. Why was this so?

Traditional moneylenders face a market in which the scarcity of finance relative to demand maintains interest rates at very high levels. The purposes for which money is borrowed at these rates are exceptional, often based on social obligations rather than commercial opportunities. Investment-oriented CIGPs add to the available supply of loanable funds, reducing the cost of borrowing and so opening up opportunities for investment that could not be justified at the

26

Thatching is still an important industry in the poverty economy

Contract harvesting. Indonesia

former higher-ruling informal rates of interest. The CIGP can, therefore, be additive rather than competitive with the traditional financial networks of the poor. The impact of the CIGP is to raise the available supply of loanable funds for investment finance so that additional investment takes place. This new investment does not displace investments to which there exist on-going commitments. CIGPs do not have to seek business by offering to re-finance investments that were profitable at the higher interest rates that previously reigned. Conflict is courted when there is a deliberate attempt to offer re-financing for projects already funded from traditional sources. CIGPs can avoid this sort of confrontation by concentrating their efforts in the additive area of investment activity. However, there may well exist cases where one may not wish to resile from this possibility. The most successful CIGPs enable local NGOs to launch income- and employment-generating development activities among the poor that add to their range of viable investment opportunities, capitalizing on un-exploited market niches that do not involve conflict-generating zero-sum games. We can use the economists' supply and demand tools of economic analysis to describe how this can be achieved. Interested readers are referred to the Appendix: The Simple Economics of CIGP, for a formal documentation.

Urban v rural programmes

If a significant impact is to be made on the alleviation of systemic poverty it is important that development initiatives are targetted at the poor. Trickle-down programmes have not worked because they are founded on the shot-gun principle — lack of targetting and little penetration. If CIGPs are to avoid making the same mistake, a sizeable effort in income and employment generation should be in the rural districts. The rapid growth of urban centres, including rural towns, is also a powerful magnet for a significant concentration of effort in urban areas.

The share of urban population in the total population of developing countries has increased from less than 7 per cent in 1920 to more than 30 per cent in 1980. By the turn of the century it is expected to approach 45 per cent (Sethuraman, 1981: v). In some developing countries, especially the poorer economies, the trend to urbanization is even faster. In only twenty years, the urban population of Bangladesh has tripled to 18 per cent in 1985, and is continuing to grow at around 8 per cent per annum. In the lowest-income developing countries as a group, the urban population growth rate during 1980–5 was 5.4 per cent per annum, compared to 3.5 per cent in the middle-income countries (World Bank, 1987). These numbers suggest two things: first, income generation through the expansion of non-farm employment opportunities is and will continue to be a critical goal in the war on poverty; second, that an increasing proportion of these jobs will need to be in the off-farm, typically urban sector of developing countries.

There is every possibility that an urban, non-farm strategy of employment generation will accelerate the growth of towns and the drift to established cities. This has a silver lining in that to the extent that it does augment these trends it also reduces unemployment in the rural economy. The consequences for those who remain on the land are also silver-lined in that average rural household income will tend to rise. This is so not only because off-farm employment can make significant inroads on rural underemployment but remittances, no matter how irregular, are a welcome injection of new cash income. The spectre of rapid population growth in rural towns and established urban areas as a result of in-migration from agriculture is not, therefore, an argument for eschewing town-based income- and employment-generation activities. It is an argument for not neglecting the considerable potential for off-farm employment generation in rural-based towns and cities.

The foregoing conclusions are further supported by the demographic trend in developing countries towards an aging but youthful population. In Brazil and many other populous developing countries, the employment problem confronting policy makers is all the more urgent because more than 40 per cent of the population is 15 years or older. It is estimated that by the year 2000, almost 800 million new jobs will have to be created just to keep pace with the numbers that will enter the workforce. Fewer than 10 per cent of these jobs are likely to be found in agriculture (Tendler, 1987:3). The only viable alternative is the millions of labour-intensive micro-enterprises and small businesses that make up the institutional fabric of poverty in the Third World.

Some common fallacies

In development circles poverty alleviation is not fashionable.
Poverty is a target, not a condition to be studied and understood. Poverty is a problem, a reason why the best-laid plans
of development planners and expatriate experts so often go
awry. In discussions of malnutrition and global starvation,
for example, while it is acknowledged that the world no longer has a food problem because there is more than enough
food to feed everyone on the planet more than adequately,
the role of poverty as a root cause of hunger is not given the
attention it deserves. Global hunger persists not because
there is not enough food to go round but because the mal-
nourished do not have the wherewithal to buy the food they
need.

If we are serious about abolishing starvation and malnutrition, we have to do much more about reducing poverty. For
this to happen there is a prior need to reassess our conventional wisdom about poverty and development as the singu-
lar lack of success that has attended the global effort to
overcome poverty in the Third World over the past four
decades indicates. Why have the global commitments of
national governments and international agencies to international economic development not achieved greater inroads in
the war on want? Is it because our preconceptions are off the
mark? Do we understand the problem of poverty well
enough?

There is very little research that has been done on the
microeconomics of the survival activities of the poor. Consequently, there is a prima facie case for questioning whether
we really do have a defensible basis on which we can claim to
know what to do about solving the problem of poverty. The
conventional wisdom is based largely on assumptions about
what it is like to be poor, the opportunities open to the poor
and the potential ability of the poor to help themselves if left
to do so. Economic growth is presented as the panacea for
poverty, the failure of economic growth to trickle down to
the poor notwithstanding. Is it the myopia of the received
wisdom that has prevented greater attention and resources
from being devoted to the mobilization of microenterprises
and poverty alleviation as alternative engines of economic
growth and development in the Third World? Could we not
reverse the reasoning and seek economic growth through

poverty alleviation, in a sort of trickle-up process? Should we not begin at the base of the Poverty Pyramid, given that our ultimate goal must be to invert the Pyramid so that the greatest number become the least poor at the top and the poorest become the least in number at the bottom? It is with these questions in mind that we explore some of the more important stock responses about poverty and development.

The poverty cringe

It is still not uncommon to experience the poverty cringe, especially in official circles, when one suggests working with the poor in the Third World. The automatic reaction is to list, consciously or unconsciously, the problems that will have to be dealt with because the poor are 'illiterate, itinerant and unaccountable'. The stock response is to deny the poor the respect and recognition that one doesn't think twice about giving a clean, well-dressed engineer, agronomist, teacher or doctor.

> The idea that the poor are themselves ultimately responsible for the backwardness and lack of progress in rural areas of the Third World is not only fairly widely accepted in Western nations but also reflects a prevalent trend of thinking among the ruling elite of the devloping world. (Schnieder, 1988:140)

Chronic poverty is a symptom of the existence of systems of injustice in our societies. No matter how much one wishes to avoid the rhetoric of the do-gooder fraternity, the reality is that the poor are victims of entrenched socio-economic systems that allow poverty to persist. There is no evidence that the poor want to be poor, nor does the evidence of many thousands of small enterprise-loan transactions indicate that the poor are less trustworthy or less likely to react in a manner consistent with rational self-interest as are wealthier and better educated persons. The poor deserve our trust and respect as business experts in their own environment; they do not need our charity or patronizing advice. Yet, the unconscious social biases and prejudices that underlie the poverty cringe are real and primary reasons why it is so easy to fall into the trap of working 'for the poor' rather than 'with the poor'.

The consequences of this trap are both subtle and profound and go a long way to explaining why poverty-alleviation programmes of the CIGP variety have not hereto contributed to development to the extent that they ought.

David Korten (1976) summarizes thus: 'In the name of helping the poor, the bureaucracies through which most development assistance is dispensed serve first their own members and then the local elites' (Korten, 1987:146). The alleviation of systemic poverty will not work as a foundation stone of Third World development unless the poor are genuinely accorded the respect and dignity they deserve as rational and essential contributors to economic activity.

The poor are a poor credit risk
Western banking practices and prejudices are the basis on which financial systems have developed in the Third World. In no area is this more evident than in the rules relating to the borrower's responsibility to furnish the lender with collateral. These rules discriminate against the poor, who have no collateral, and are applied with rigid faith in the corollary that it is riskier to lend to the asset poor than the asset rich. This faith is applied irrationally, with no apparent concession to whether the repayment record of the poor is as bad as this assumption implies (see Croucher and Gupta, 1988; Farnsworth, 1988; Harper, 1979; Levitsky and Prasad, 1987). Consequently formal banking systems in the Third World do not service the financial needs of the poor because they believe it would be bad for their profitability.

It is foolhardy to suggest that lending to the poor is not risky. Any form of lending activity carries risks but from what evidence there is available it is not true that it is any more risky to lend to the poor than to the rich. The opposite may well be the case. An official in Sri Lanka told me that the on-time repayment rate on government guaranteed loans in that country averaged not more than 7 per cent in the 1980s. This compares to an average on-time repayment for the CIGPs examined in this study that exceeds 90 per cent! A similar gap favouring the poor exists between the loan default rate experienced by banks and other modern-sector lending institutions and the default rate on CIGP loans. Repayment records for CIGPs reported in the literature and studied for this book confirm this remarkable result. The data give us reason to be confident in our belief that there is profit to be had in helping the poor to help themselves (see Ashe, 1985; Bolnick, 1987; Farbman, 1981; Jacobi, 1988). Yet the poor continue to be denied access to formal credit channels, justified by a persistent belief that they are a poor credit risk.

The poor are stuck in a poverty trap

In a similar vein, it is commonly held that the poor remain poor because they are stuck in a poverty trap. The trap is sustained because there is a lack of adequately profitable economic opportunities available to the poor or to those who service their consumption needs. Only the big-push of a government-backed integrated development programme can overcome the depressed economic condition that causes poverty to be chronic. The poverty-trap thesis enshrines the notion that poverty is too big a problem for anything but government intervention to overcome.

The poverty trap is also characterized in the conventional wisdom by low productivity which keeps wages low and demand for commodities modest if not mean. Low incomes entrench the depressed state of the poor by preventing profitable investment opportunities from arising, scotching any possibility that survival-level incomes might form the basis of a private-sector initiated, demand-led escape from poverty. What's more, because incomes are so low, the poor are perceived as being unable to accumulate adequate savings to finance a viable business venture.

Anecdotal evidence and what data there are on how the poor survive, what they do to earn their income and what they do with their incomes contradict the conclusions suggested by the poverty-trap thesis (see Sethuraman, 1981:29–36 especially). Average productivity in enterprises run by the poor is low but the response of productivity to even quite small investments can be dramatic. Demand for commodities by the poor is also highly sensitive to income changes, so that the multiplier effect on growth in income from strategic pump-priming in support of income- and employment-generation projects can be very large. And the poor do save, but in very small amounts at any one time. Their problem is not that they cannot save but that they are unable to save enough or in a way that will allow the accumulation of the real value of savings which when put on deposit can then be drawn on to fund the investment opportunities available to them.

The challenge for the operators of CIGPs and the borrowers from these programmes is two-fold. First to find ways to ensure that the savings of the poor are mobilized and effectively invested, without imposing procedures and bureaucratic niceties that generate excessive transaction costs.

If CIGPs can provide the poor with an outlet for their savings that provides a capital-guaranteed reward for their frugality (that is, a rate of return in excess of inflation), a critical step will have been taken to destroy the conditions that can and do make poverty a trap for so many in the world today. Second, the savings of the poor must be complemented by appropriate levels of credit finance. The lending policy of the CIGP must be related to savings capacity of the intending borrower.

What is good for the nation is good for the poor
It is difficult to adjudicate on the proper role of government in a targetted poverty-alleviation first strategy of development planning because so few Third World governments have ever tried it! Government development projects are, in the main, macroeconomic in their design and dependent on ripple effects, the trickle-down of benefits, for their impact on poverty. Moreover, the appropriate role of government is often clouded by such statements as, 'What is good for the nation is good for the poor'. In fact, although government-sponsored economic growth initiatives in the formal modern economy in Third World countries can be unequivocally good for the nation, the benefits of economic growth in the modern sector of poor economies largely bypass those who find their livelihood in the survival enterprises of the poor. Untargetted macroeconomic growth has done little to relive the poor of their burden. For economic growth to be of benefit to them it has to be economic growth of a different sort from that which flows from a strategy of development through modernization.

The benefits of economic growth in the formal sectors of Third World economies tend to bypass the poor because modern-sector development projects, even those that are designated projects of national significance, do little to improve the productivity of the poor. A new power plant, a new hospital, improved seaport facilities, a new airport terminal or a new timber mill may augment the standard of living of bureaucrats, the captains of industry, skilled workers and professionals in the formal workforce, but will make barely a difference to the value-added generated by the firms that employ the poor, produce for the poor and sell to the poor.

Poverty-alleviation targetted development projects are distinguished by the fact that they make a frontal attack on poverty, seeking to improve output per person and the total value of production from enterprises of the poor. The typical approach to development projects does not, however, follow this path. Consider, for example, the steps that are likely to go into the implementation of a handicrafts-oriented development project. The stated aim of the project is to provide employment for poor people by exploiting the national and international markets that the project sponsors believe exist for local handicrafts. For the sake of argument, let us assume that government backing for the project is forthcoming because governments give a high priority to employment generation for the poor and are especially keen to also support projects able to generate foreign exchange from handicraft exports and sales to foreigners in the lucrative total tourist market.

As a first step a handicrafts export organization is established, with government backing in the form of exclusive licences to conduct and regulate the trade and subsidies to cover what are presented as high transport and set-up costs because the handicrafts are sourced from producers in remote villages. Benefits to the poor are seen as flowing from the injection of regular cash flow from sales to the programme principals. Upon enquiry we find that the handicrafts are purchased from producers in the villages at prices that are competitive with what local consumers pay in local markets. Some discount may even be demanded by the principals in return for firm bulk-orders that provide the basis of guaranteed long-term employment in the village. Alternatively, the programme may deliberately seek to change the nature of the handicrafts trade by giving higher priority to improving the prices realized by village producers and so offer a premium for quality or for products produced with characteristics that are judged most saleable.

The next steps in the programme require the handicrafts collected from the villages to pass through several stages of processing to bring them up to export quality. This may be no more demanding than sorting and pricing or it may extend to washing and cleaning in the case of textiles, sanding, polishing and painting in the case of cane or rattan furniture, sorting according to size, colour or some other specification labelling and packaging. This processing adds value to the product and forms the base price on which the the retail profit margin is calculated. Typically this margin can far exceed the total amount that has found its way into the pay-packets of poor and largely unskilled workers in the informal economy. The lion's share of the revenue from sales goes not to the village producers nor to those who prepare the product for exort and sale, but to the project principals, their distributors and the exporters. Has the project advanced the cause of poverty alleviation? Has the productivity of the poor and the value-added coming from village production been increased?

These are critical questions, the answers to which are not always obvious or simple. In Indonesia and the Philippines the furniture trade is an important handicraft industry. However, officials there lamented that the cane and rattan furniture export trade has driven up prices and caused an over-exploitation of rattan resources but not led to a significant improvement of income for village producers and raw material suppliers. The poor can no longer afford traditional rattan furniture nor is there sustained employment in the trade. Is this a contribution to their welfare and well-being? Similarly infrastructure projects that promote the tourist trade (such as hotels, resorts, air and sea terminal facilities) with a view to increasing local employment and foreign exchange earnings can have perverse effects that impact especially on the poor. Demand from the hotels forces up prices of locally supplied produce, such as fish, fruit and vegetables, beyond the budget of the poor. The representatives of a CIGP servicing the credit needs of the poorest of the poor in Valenzuela, a poor district on the outskirts of Manila, Philippines, commented that government commitments to tourism, and harbour development to service local industries, had meant that fresh seafood has largely disappeared from the diet of the poor slum dwellers because it has become too expensive. The poor do not find it easy to secure a substitute for such a traditional and ready source of protein. A much neglected but critically important feature of CIGPs is that they largely avoid these perverse side effects because the CIGPs target the poor directly, raise the productivity of the poor directly and through the focus on wage-goods production and distribution increase the flow of value-added of direct benefit to the poor.

Small business is big business in less developed countries

The poor in less developed countries (LDCs) are either self-employed, employed by small family-businesses or sell their labour on an itinerant basis as unskilled day-wage or piece workers. Based on enquiries made in each of the seven countries visited for field-work for this study, there seems to be a consistent rate at which day-wage labour is remunerated. It does not greatly matter whether the so-called unskilled work undertaken is as a casual domestic servant doing the washing and ironing, various 'goffer' employments handling mail and messages, security guard duty, gardening, day-labour in agriculture or manual work of one sort or another on building sites, around factories or in recycling enterprises — the wage paid rarely falls far from the dollar-a-day mark. This is a very meagre wage on which only those born to poverty know how to survive. Many do survive, but they do not find it easy nor is their life expectancy long. Marginal improvements in their situation and prospects, such as a small increase in their earnings, let's say of 20–50 cents per day, can make a substantial difference to their savings capacity, the range of opportunities they are able to realize and their personal dignity. Nowhere is this better demonstrated than in the experiences of poor people in Dominique Lapierre's (1986) best-selling epic *The City of Joy*, Buchi Emecheta's (1979) moving account in *The Joys of Motherhood* and Kamala Markandaya's (1954) Indian classic *Nectar in a Sieve*.

The daily earnings of a self-employed worker in one of the many areas of enterprise that provide the poor with a livelihood are well above those offered to members of the vulnerable or labouring poor. These daily earnings are in effect the own-wage paid to oneself. The own-wage invariably exceeds the unskilled wage rate, often by a factor of several magnitudes (see Mazumdar, 1976:662–6). This margin is a reflection of two primary factors: there are always more people chasing jobs than there are persons capable of creating their own job; and the higher productivity of these small business-entrepreneurs over that of their employed co-residents in poverty supports a high remuneration. To the extent that more of the vulnerable and labouring poor are not self-employed because a finance constraint prevents them from starting up in business, for example, as an owner-driver rickshaw operator, in food processing or vending, as a household implement or furniture maker, a manufactured-component fabricator or processor, a garment maker or shopkeeper of one sort or another, productivity in the informal economy of the poor is lower than it could be.

CIGPs are an important way of loosening this credit constraint, that allows both the productivity and the total household income of the poor to increase significantly. What we do not know is by how much productivity would rise if the finance constraint were no greater than it is in the formal modern sector of Third World economies. The limited data there are on the internal rate of return to projects that provide credit to informal-sector microenterprises indicate that the impact can confidently be expected to be quite large, certainly in excess of the 10 per cent opportunity cost that the World Bank and other financial institutions seek to achieve in their development-lending programmes.

Household firms or microenterprises are the cornerstone of economic activity in the earliest stages of development. As the economy progresses from low to higher levels of average GNP per head of population, the proportion of firms that exist at the household level tends to decline. But when the economy is still at the low end of the GNP per head spectrum, small, essentially household firms, including smallholder farms, are the primary source of employment and output. This is evident from the cross-country historical data in Table 1.2, which confirm the very important place that small enterprises hold in developing countries.

Table 1.2 Percentage of manufacturing employment in household* firms

	1953	1961	1967	1969	1970	1971	1973	1975	1977
Colombia	59	–	–	–	54	–	49	–	43
Ghana	–	–	–	–	78	–	–	–	–
India (Uttar Pradesh)†	–	–	–	–	–	60	–	–	–
Indonesia	–	–	–	–	–	–	–	76	–
Kenya	–	–	–	49	–	–	–	–	–
Philippines	–	–	63	–	–	–	–	53	–
Tanzania	–	–	55	–	–	–	–	–	–
Turkey	–	–	–	–	55	–	–	–	50
Japan	35	15	–	–	15	–	17	19	–

Sources: Anderson, 1982, Tables 1–2 and Fig. 1; Biggs and Oppenheim, 1986, Tables 1.2 and 1.3.

* Includes self-employed and family workers in firms of not more than 5 employees.
† Single worker and not more than 10 employees.

It is in the interests of the poor that the number of household firms should increase. A number of these same firms must also be nurtured beyond the confines of their smallness if sufficient jobs are to be created to absorb the number of poor people entering the workforce annually. CIGPs have proved an effective means of supporting both goals.

Characteristics of household and other small enterprises

The importance of household and small firms to the welfare of the poor cannot be gauged just from the contribution they make to employment of the poor. We must also look at other characteristics of these firms, in particular ways in which these microenterprises are different from the private enterprises in the formal modern economy in Third World countries. There are 10 distinguishing features that are especially important.

o The first important difference we find concerns women. The formal sector in developing economies places women at a distinct disadvantage in the employment and prosperity stakes. Modern business practice pays a premium to those with education. Women are typically the last in line to acquire even simple numeracy and literacy skills, if ever they are given the opportunity. Businesses, public-sector enterprise and government bureaucracies also prefer to employ persons able to conform to regular office hours but the lack of child-minding facilities, a myriad of other household responsibilities and culutral or religious restrictions prevent women from competing on equal terms in the market place. Household and larger microenterprises do not have the same biases as formal-sector firms. Microenterprises lend themselves to more flexible work hours and arrangements that enable women to participate without disadvantage because of their traditional homemaker and child-rearing roles.

o Many enterprises in the informal poverty economy rely on the application of skills learned from traditional domestic duties of women and children, especially those associated with food processing, laundry, textile crafts, baset making and weaving with bamboo or other grasses. The call for the products of these activities is as ubiquitous and reliable as is demand for wage-goods anywhere. Consequently, these firms are uniquely placed to employ and benefit from those who are among the least advantaged peoples in the Third World, women and children. It should not come as a surprise, therefore, that the primary borrowers and beneficiaries of CIGP loans are women and other members of the vulnerable poor. A high proportion of small businesses and household firms is owned by women and they have a tendency to employ family members and/or other women to help them. Blayney and Otero (1985:10) report that in Asia and Central America more than half the 5,000-odd firms surveyed employing up to 4 persons, including the owner, were owned by women. The Programme for Investment in the Small Capital Enterprise Sector (PISCES) case-studies from Africa, Latin America and Asia (which covered much smaller samples of often smaller firms engaged in survival activities at the very bottom of the economic ladder) found that women owned and operated between two-thirds and three-quarters of the microenterprises given a loan (see Ashe, 1985:11). The PISCES findings are in line with those encountered in our own field-work for this study.

○ Household firms and microenterprises are small scale and highly flexible, designed to exploit market opportunities when and where they arise. Part-time employment is an important feature of their flexibility.

○ Economic activity in the informal economy is uniquely labour intensive with a similarly unique potential to create a large number of sustained jobs for the poor much more cheaply than any competing sector in the economy. The experience of a large number of CIGPs confirms that even quite small investments in enterprises producing to service the needs of the poor can create a permanent job in market niches where demand justifies the investment: 'A survey of tinsmiths, carpenters, cobblers, mattress makers, and tailors in Nairobi showed an average of $15 investment' (Ashe, 1985:3).

○ Microenterprises are local-market oriented servicing, in the main, the needs of consumers and investors who are simultaneously residents in poverty and suppliers of inputs into the production processes of their neighbours. The goods and services produced are typically traditional wage-goods, the demand for which is fairly stable. Productivity gains that result in lower prices to consumers spread the benefit even further.

○ Each microenterprise supports a large number of dependants — for the projects we visited there were rarely less than 5 persons per owner, not including employees, dependent for their livelihood on the success of the family-based enterprise.

> The difference in earning a dollar a day to meet the needs of an average family of 5–8, and $2 a day is dramatic: children may be sent to school, the sick can see a doctor, housing can be upgraded, and it becomes possible to save for future investment in the business. (Farbman, 1981:35)

This is not trickle-down; it is an immediate transfusion against the worst deprivations of poverty.

○ Small businesses are almost wholly funded from family savings plus small loans from informal moneylenders (see Liedholm and Mead, 1987:118 especially). Household firms and microenterprises supplying wage-goods to the local market are often one of the few avenues of investment open to the poor that pay a positive real rate of return. Bank desposits, if they are accepted from the poor, pay deposit rates that typically fall far short of the local inflation rate, account management fees notwithstanding. It remains true that the savings of the poor are small in absolute terms which, combined with their lack of access to formal banking-sector credit and investment finance systems, tends to keep them chained to outmoded technology.

○ The businesses that provide the poor with paid employment are also a major source of on-the-job training in rudimentary manufacturing and craft skills not otherwise available to the poor. This can be especially important where new technologies are involved and traditional apprenticeships not readily available. Examples include the manufacture of plastic goods, fibre-glass based products, metal working and electronics.

○ A universal characteristic of household and microenterprise firms is their irregular and often illegal character. Survival of informal poverty-economy enterprises often depends upon the ability to ignore government regulations. These may concern registration requirements, tax avoidance, the application of minimum wage laws, minimum safety standards and general work conditions, procedures intended to ensure basic product quality and hygiene standards, packaging requirements, warranties and reporting standards. Hernando de Soto (1987) goes so far as to equate the informal poverty economy with the 'illegal sector': [it is] virtually impossible for poor people . . . to live and work legally . . . the costs of remaining legal are overwhelming' (p.2).

It is commonly remarked that household firms and microenterprises survive in spite of rather than with the help of government policy and regulation. As a result there appears to be a vast untapped gain to be had, of immediate and direct benefit to the poor from the design and implementation of policies that are more sensitive and supportive of the private-enterprise endeavours of the poor. Even where policy makers have 'addressed the supposed need for cheap loans by low income entrepreneurs, they have ignored how the policies and programmes they have created undermine the viability of these firms and the financial institutions created to make these loans' (Meyer, 1988:17).

○ The high cost of borrowed capital in the informal poverty economy is well above that available in the formal banking sector in Third World countries. In order to be able to service these loans the enterprise investments of the poor have to be far more profitable than investments by firms in the modern sector. Chandavarkar (1988) quotes figures for Africa that suggest a real rate of return to own-savings and funds borrowed from relatives of 15–25 per cent for investments funded from CIGPs (p.12). Loans from moneylenders are not only expensive but tend to be restricted to small amounts, often too small to stimulate significantly business growth and subject to repayment schedules too short to finance investment in long-term assets. Consequently there is reason to believe there is considerable underinvestment in legitimate business opportunities in the poverty sector (see Farbman, 1981). A USAID-funded study of 12 industry groups, undertaken by Michigan State University, compared the 'economic efficiency' of small and large firms in similar industries. The results indicated that, 'in 10 out of 12 specific industry groups examined, the social benefit-cost ratios of the small firms . . . are greater than the comparable ratios for the large scale firms in those particular industries and countries' (Liedholm and Mead, 1987:120).

The important corollary to the observation that firms of the poor are starved of capital and pay high real rates of interest is that subsidized credit is not essential to correct the market failure that denies the poor access to formal credit channels. Household and small businesses are more than able to pay commercial interest rates, if only monies at these rates were available. The greatest financial constraint facing these enterprises is access to finance, not the price at which it might be had. In the majority of cases the real rate of interest faced by the poor is infinity because access to medium- to long-term loanable funds is zero. It does not come as a surprise, therefore, that one of the key reasons forwarded by programme personnel for why repayment rates of CIGPs for the poor are so close to 100 per cent is concern by small entrepreneurs to retain their access to eligibility for repeat loans (see Anderson and Khambata, 1985:362; Ashe, 1985a:8–10,45,130; Farbman, 1981:xii; Kahnert, 1987:39; Swincer, 1988:11; USAID, 1985:118). Access to credit at market rates of interest is the asset that entrepreneurs in poverty are denied. Once they gain access to this asset they will go to remarkable lengths to protect it.

The importance of liquidity and access to credit

The poor live predominantly in a cash economy. Their lifestyle is not that of the traditional villager or peasant farmer at peace with the environment and in equilibrium with the subsistence economy of old. The poor tend to be displaced, out of equilibrium in a socio-economic environment in which money and not barter is the currency of exchange for survival. They are typically landless, often without a fixed address, lacking the facilities to store more than the barest minimum of the necessities of life. At the edge of survival they are committed, by necessity, to a lifestyle that maximizes their flexibility and ability to take advantage of every economic opportunity that comes their way. The significance of the observation that the poor have too little money is critical.

In this study we concentrate our attention on those programmes targetted at loosening the finance constraint that plagues the poor microenterprise entrepreneur. Our reason is simple, intuitively appealing and consistent with the evidence that even casual observation reveals. In even the meanest situations in the Third World there is no lack of vendors seeking to sell the essentials of life: food, clothing, shelter, health, education and companionship. The problem that prevents the poor from translating their desires into effective demand is the lack of cash income. It is the central hypothesis of this study, therefore, that a key obstacle to poverty alleviation in the Third World is the restrictions imposed by the lack of access to investment finance. Primary suport for this proposition can be found in Sen's (1980, 1981) pioneering work on poverty as the outcome of a deprivation of 'entitlements'; further support comes from Michael Lipton (1988) in his most useful World Bank Discussion Paper, 'The poor and the poorest', where Lipton identifies 'low outlay or income per person' as an accurate broad-brush measure of poverty' (p. 47).

The finance constraint is also critical because inadequate working capital prevents poor and small entrepreneurs from expanding the range of goods they can produce (and thereby the employment they offer), restricts the stock they can carry or prevents them from being able to supply on credit to develop and exploit new market opportunities. The lack of access to finance is a key constraint to the creation of new wealth by entrepreneurs who seek to service the needs of consumers who are poor but nonetheless buyers in the market place. The daily liquidity crisis with which the poor must contend acts as a halter on initiative, restricting the spread of self-reliant development. Denial of access by the poor to loans from modern-sector banks and financial institutions aggravates the 'paradox of thrift' in the economy of the poverty sector, further constraining what limited prospects there are for the poor to share in the material benefits of economic development.

The poor face almost total denial of access to formal credit facilities, especially in developing countries. This restricts their investment activities to what can be financed from personal savings or to those investments that are so essential or so highly profitable as to bear the cost of restrictive if not usurious interest rates (rates of 10 per cent per day and more are not unusual), offered by informal moneylenders. These interest rates mean that the poor borrow only when it is critical to do so and are restricted to small amounts loaned for brief periods from private informal moneylenders adept at the exploitation of their monopoly power.

A neglected but critical constraint facing the poor is the lack of institutions able to assist them to mobilize their own savings for their own benefit. In the formal modern economy banks fulfil this basic, intermediation role, but in the deprived socio-economic environment in which the poor operate, if the banks accept savings from the poor (often they will not because the amounts are so small as to leave no margin to cover transaction costs), these monies are recycled to borrowers able to meet collateral and other bureaucratic requirements. It may not be unfair to say that institutions able to play a similar intermediation or banking role on behalf of the poor are even more scarce than are the savings of the poor.

The lack of institutions willing to offer financial services to the poor has an unintended but very real impact on liquidity in the economics of poverty. In a cash-starved economy the rate at which money circulates is a vital element influencing the money supply available to the poor. The more frequently money changes hands in a given period of time the greater is the effective money supply and the less onerous the liquidity or finance constraint. Whenever a bank or other financial institution accepts deposits from a poor depositor, however, typically this money is not recycled back into the economy in which the poor live. The very success of the bank in mobilizing the savings of poor people to whom they will then not lend merely exacerbates the liquidity problems that contriubte in such an important way to keeping the poor poor.

Since modern banks deny loans to any potential borrower who cannot meet its modern-sector oriented borrowing requirements, there is a leekage of liquidity available to the poor. The result is not only a fall in the supply of loanable funds available to poor households and microenterprises servicing the needs of the poor but also a fall in the velocity of circulation of money. These two combine to force a rise in interest rates that the poor must pay to informal moneylenders for short-term cash.

There is a preconception that there are no profitable investment opportunities in the world of the chronically poor. If this be true it remains for us to explain why the village-level moneylenders can do business at the rates they are able to charge? The answer lies in the realities of the supply and demand for loanable funds available to the poor.

If one lists in cumulative order the range of investment opportunities available to the poor, we find that there are very few investments that offer a very high rate of return but a much larger number that offer a lower rate of return. In other words, there are very many fewer highly profitable projects than the number of not so profitable projects. The demand for finance by potential investors in microenterprises servicing the needs of the poor is determined by the interest rate they have to pay for finance relative to the profitability of the investment opportunities available to them. The higher is that rate of interest the lower the volume of investment that can be justified by prospective profits, and vice versa. If the supply of finance available to the poor could be increased as a result of an injection of new credit to microenterprises by an NGO-operated CIGP programme, the rate of interest demanded of poor people would fall and the level of viable investment opportunities open to the poor would increase. This higher level of investment will typically be associated with increased employment, plus an increase in productivity and/or value-added within enterprises serving the consumption and income needs of the poor. Moreover, the increase in investment can be expected to have a 'multiplier' effect of substantial proportions as the income generated by the new employment enlivens the spending cycle in the Poverty Sector.

Liquidity leakages have an opposite effect to that of a credit injection. If there is a leakage brought on, let us assume, by the introduction of a government-sponsored household small-savings mobilization programme, the supply of loanable funds (that is, credit) falls with the new equilibrium between the demand for loanable funds and the supply settling at a higher rate of interest and a lower level of investment. Hence, the bank deposits of the poor that are not recycled to the poor, are a leakage that exacerbates the chronic liquidity shortage always facing the poor, making it even more difficult for poor entrepreneurs operating microenterprises to invest and generate jobs than it was before. It is critical that if CIGP programmes are to avoid this perverse result of a bank-linked programme, they must obtain guarantees that the co-operating banks will recycle savings deposits by the poor to borrowers from poor households. (See the

'Appendix: The Simple Economics of CIGP', for a more formal statement of these propositions.)

It is often not in the formal banking system's interests to reach out to the poor. Banks are there to provide a service and make a profit from so doing. It is logical that they should choose first to meet the finance needs of their most important customers. These customers the banks identify after considering the client–bank relationship against security offered to underwrite the loan, risks associated with the venture for which the loan is sought, ability of the potential borrower to meet specific bureaucratic contractual requirements, and commercial project viability criteria. There is, therefore, an understandable preference on the part of banks to favour borrowers who are the local captains of industry, with collateral and other trappings of a monetized society sought by modern-sector financial lending institutions, (i.e., a fixed address, ability to read and write, etc.). As the prefered exemplars of modernity, local captains of industry also appeal to the banks as clients because they are often in a position to secure, for the benefit of the bank, a government loan guarantee, or they are clients of political importance whom the banks judge well placed to advance their own corporate future (such as government instrumentalities or major corporations with political clout). Once these loans are serviced there may be very little left in the kitty, no matter how impressive a savings record the also-rans have been able to establish.

If we begin in equilibrium at the rate of interest i^*, the level of investment i^* that can be financed results in a level of employmnt, n^*, which at the going wage rate, w, generates an income flow to the poor of y^*. After the introduction of CIGP, the supply of loanable funds increases and a new equilibrium is reached at a lower rate of interest, $r\dagger$. At this lower rate the level of investment that can be financed profitably increases by $i^*i\dagger$, which in turn increases the demand for labour by $n^*n\dagger$. At the going wage rate, w, the increase in employment results in an increase in income received by the poor of $y^*y\dagger$, which equals the increase in employment, $n^*n\dagger$, multiplied by the wage rate, w.

The problem of transactions costs and collateral

It would be remiss if we did not say a few words on the importance of transactions costs and the restrictive requirement of collateral. The formal banking system is impersonal and depends on various structured information-gathering and verification procedures to select those to whom it will lend from those to whom it will not. These procedures demand not only literacy but also documentation and time. These requirements are not costless, either to the banking agency or the potential client. Consequently, the poor tend to miss out all round.

In the main the very poor need only small loans, loans so small that the interest rate the banks would need to charge in order to recover the transactions costs that their systems of doing business involve could easily exceed the amount borrowed by several factors. For example, if the bank's transactions costs per loan made amount to a fixed charge of \$10 plus a variable component of 20¢ for every \$10 borrowed, then a loan of only \$100 would need to charge 12 per cent per annum to break even. A profit margin of a modest 10 per cent per annum brings the interest rate that the bank would need to charge to meet its opportunity costs to 22 per cent. If the current bank interest rate sanctioned by the government is set at a maximum below this level, let's say only 15 per cent per annum, the bank cannot make a profit on small loans. There is a strong incentive for the bank to service the larger borrowing needs of customers who also offer the bank the highest margin above its transaction costs. Inevitably the poor are not high on this priority list.

The research reported in this study indicates that on the lender's side there are ways in which the transactions costs on small loans can be reduced. If the banks are willing to be innovative in how they handle these transactions costs, the potential profit margin on such loans justifies a much higher place on their priority list than the application of current formal banking practices shows as warranted. Moreover, the appropriate financial intermediation services that are the missing link in current systems may require the co-operation of indigenous NGOs, willing and able to relieve the banks of the need to cling to traditional bureaucratic procedures. The intermediation that such NGOs could play would be to work on behalf of groups of small borrowers in order to do the following:

○ utilize what economies of scale there are to reduce transactions costs

○ offer the banks a cost effective alternative means of identifying borrowers of good standing
○ select potential borrowers with viable proposals; and
○ establish a reliable mechanism for ensuring on-time loan repayments and for dealing with loan defaulters. Current banking practices seek to achieve all these ends but at a transaction cost that in the context of very small loans, often less than $100, neither the banks nor their potential borrowers among the poor can afford.

At the client level, the critical transaction cost confronting the poor is the time-intensive nature of borrowing from the formal banking sector. The poor survive by selling their labour, which they cannot do if they must queue and wait in line for an interview with successive bank officials, spend time seeking out the correct form to be completed, find and possibly pay for a suitable person to help fill in the plethora of forms associated with modern-sector borrowing procedures, queue some more for costly birth certificates or other identity papers required by the loan clerk, plus arrange and pay for the preparation of personal photos, transcripts from referees and do the needful to otherwise establish one's bona fides. For the poor, and especially the vulnerable and labouring poor at the base of the Poverty Pyramid, the opportunity cost of the time and money that this process consumes is often nothing short of survival. A day's wages lost can make all the difference when one lives at the edge of existence. Money at 10 per cent per week from the local moneylender soon looks cheap compared to bank money that you may not get, despite all the effort of trying.

Modern banking in the Third World is also only user-friendly to those able to proffer the required collateral. A banker I interviewed in Manila explained that if a client came seeking a working capital overdraft facility, the bank would require the client to keep on deposit an amount equal to the drawing right. In Nairobi another banker said much the same thing when he explained that his bank basically only lends to people who already have money. This does not describe the poor. The poor want to borrow in order to make the money which they presently do not have to offer as collateral; nor do the poor often have the next best form of collateral preferred by the banks in the Third World, title to property.

Programmes of finance for the poor must adapt to these realities. Lenders to the poor, and especially the very poor, have to adopt different, less costly methods of ensuring that investment loans are allocated to the right borrowers and that the right set of social pressures and inducements operate to ensure on-time repayment from those without collateral. Effective procedures have to be identified that minimize the transaction costs that are, in the first instance, borne by the lender in modern banking systems. This study has sought pointers to the alternative methods and procedures available. As will be seen below, these include successful experiments by many indigenous NGOs in substituting the peer-group pressure of a self-help or solidarity group for collateral to ensure high rates of loan repayment by the poor. Nonetheless, those implementing credit for the poor programmes may need to make it known that, despite the smallness of the loans being made, defaulters will be pursued through the courts, cost not withstanding, should this be necessary.

The results of this study offer some important surprises. Contrary to the implications too easily drawn from the theory of the poverty trap, the poor do have profitable investment opportunities from which to choose; the poor can save, even if very little; and they do invest their money. As clients to whom one lends money, the poor also prove to be a very good risk, disciplined by social pressure and the deeply felt need to protect their access to loanable funds for repeat business. Lending to the poor is also a socially profitable thing to do. There are only a few studies in this area but they uniformly show cost–benefit ratios and internal rates of return well in excess of those for more traditional development projects. One key conclusion of this study which relates directly to the characteristics of success, that was our goal from the outset and to which we have been unerringly drawn, should not come as a complete surprise: among the poor, financial institutions or credit-based income-generation programmes that mimic the style and procedures, but not the greed, of private moneylenders have been more successful than those that have not done so.

Laundry for local households is an important business. Nepal

Transport: a valuable service that employs many. Java, Indonesia

2: Models and examples of CIGPs

THE LESSONS WE have learnt and seek to impart here are taken, with few exceptions, from a cross-section of NGO programmes examined for this study. Each programme uses a variety of models to deliver loans to the poor. These models share a number of common characteristics, some of which could be described as top-down and others bottom-up, but each in its own right falls between the extremes of what can be described as a continuum, from top-down paternalism (which does not work), through to bottom-up self-help in action (which can work if lopped and bound by accountability restraints). The degree of success that appears to be associated with each model varies not so much with the model itself as with the extent to which the programme was planned and implemented as a collaborative enterprise by the poor for the poor. More than any other factor, success is linked with the extent to which the client group participates in and even 'owns' the programme and takes responsibility for its health and future progress.

One important way in which one can identify where in the top-down–bottom-up continuum any particular model rests is to look at how the programme handles transaction costs. These are the costs incurred during the proposal-vetting process, including assessment of project viability and applicant references, implementation of loan administration and institution of loan-repayment mechanisms. The greater the extent to which these programme transaction costs are borne by the lending agency, that is, internalized, the more top-down the programme; the greater the degree of externalization of transaction costs, that is, transaction costs are not passed on to the individual borrower but are borne by the community from which the borrowers are drawn, the more bottom-up the programme.

Modern banking systems are top-down because they involve loan application, administration and repayment systems that internalize all the transaction costs associated with lending and attempt to pass these on to individual borrowers. They are passed on from lender to borrower in the form of collateral requirements, formal contractual arrangements, procedural demands in the loan-application process, specific transaction fees and the interest rate demanded. Taken together, only substantial borrowers can afford to truck with such a lender. The cash-poor microenterprise entrepreneur who has no collateral to speak of, may not have a fixed address, is likely to be illiterate and cannot really afford to waste the time that these procedures entail is effectively filtered out. Bottom-up programmes differ in that they seek to make both the borrower and the peer/reference group from which the borrower comes part of the administrative system, spreading the cost, risks and the responsibilities for loan vetting, administration, repayment and programme disciplinary procedures across the whole community or group involved in the programme.

In addition to the importance of transaction costs, field visits by myself to programmes in 7 countries and an extensive review of the relevant literature have suggested other critical characteristics for distinguishing one model of CIGP from another. For example, does the progamme operate through individuals or groups? Is credit offered only on a conditional basis that links eligibility to demonstrated saving capacity or some other requirement? What is the primary source of programme drive and vision? Does the programme have a single goal or a range of goals going beyond the efficient and effective provision of credit? These additional considerations have been brought to bear in the identification of the three generic classes of models.

There is a plethora of models that could be described along the top-down–bottom-up continuum. I am not convinced, however, that a comprehensive taxonomic exercise to fill out the continuum serves a sufficiently significant purpose to warrant the effort. The models described below (pp. 53–60) are chosen for their representative character of the many individual models that could be distinguished. Each class of model is identified by one or more key feature. Each group of models does, nonetheless, share characteristics also found in one or more of the other groups of models, though the hybridization process is far more important across models within a group than across groups. The more significant of these common characteristics are as follows:

o Each group of models incorporates a 'revolving credit fund' as the basis for its lending capacity. An important function of the partner NGO or sponsoring official aid agency is to provide the funds needed to get this fund going and then participate in its growth by becoming a non-borrowing contributor. In some cases the partner's financial contribution is limited to a once-off cash injection, with the on-going partnership restricted to training, management assistance of various sorts or collaboration on the design and implementation of a longer-term viability strategy for the indigenous programme.

o They all share a common goal to foster the capacity of individuals to help themselves. In the process of helping themselves they help one another too.

o A given NGO programme may utilize more than one model of credit delivery and microenterprise support, especially where the CIGP is operating simultaneously in more than one area of activity. Each CIGP is free to segment its target groups and to use the model it feels is most appropriate to the client in question. Hence, the provision of loans to expand an existing microenterprise is typically operated using a different model from that tailored to loans for the creation of new microenterprises. CIGP programmes are not restricted to plumbing for the use of a single model from a particular group of models.

o The purpose of each model is not to lay down rigid rules or procedures that must be followed; rather, each model has heuristic value that ought to assist in understanding what is often observed in the field or read in anecdotal material as confusion, serendipity or the result of specific qualities of personalities involved rather than programme strength.

The key types of CIGP models are of nine basic sorts in three broad groups, called the pure-credit group, the savings-linked credit group and the welfare-oriented credit group. The models that belong to each group are shown in Table 2.1. The three groups reflect the range of aims and assumptions about the client community being targetted. It is at the individual model level that the manner in which transaction costs are handled is revealed.

Table 2.1 Types of CIGP models by group

Pure-credit group	Savings-linked credit group	Welfare-oriented credit group
Personal integrity model (a1)	Solidarity-group model (b1)	Community-development model (c1)
Umbrella model (a2)	RoSCA model (b2)	Broker model (c2)
Board-driven model (a3)	Credit-cooperative model (b3)	Merchant model (c3)

Pure-credit group

The three primary models in this group deliver finance for productive purposes to borrowers unable to borrow from formal lending institutions. The personal integrity model operates at the individual level, the umbrella model at the group level and the board-driven model at either or both. They are minimalist models in that in each there is no deliberate attempt to train the borrowers to be better business operators or to second guess the viability of investment proposals brought forward for funding by loan applicants. Transaction costs are minimized by reliance on character references from, for example, the local priest, minister, mullah, doctor or respected educator. Little or no attempt is made to assess the business ventures submitted for funding. Trust is placed in the judgement of the referee, plus the self-discipline that flows from concern among potential borrowers not to spoil their market and lose continuing access to this source of investment finance. At the individual level we call this the personal integrity model. It is one of three models used by the Maha Bhoga Marga Foundation (MBM) to run its small-enterprise support programme in Bali, Indonesia.

The minimalist strategy of the pure-credit group has been effectively used not only to help individual entrepreneurs whom referees judge trustworthy but also umbrella groups that represent a membership with common interests. North of Jogjakarta, Indonesia, there is an association of persons involved in various aspects of the motor-vehicle wrecking, recovery, repair and recycling industry. From the thousands of small enterprises that make up the industry, garages and repair shops purchase spare parts for cars, trucks, buses and motorcycles. The association borrows money on behalf of its members from a local NGO, the Indonesian Welfare

55

Foundation (YIS), and then on-lends the money to members at rates of interest that are profitable, above the formal bank-lending rate, yet well below the rates charged by informal moneylenders. Individual association members are not eligible to borrow from the banks so they are more than happy to avail themselves of working capital loans through the association programme. The association uses its profits to assist members in difficulty and ensure that repayment obligations to YIS are fulfilled.

The motor-vehicle wreckers and recyclers association represents thousands of owner-operators whose livelihoods depend on the ability to pay cash for unroadworthy vehicles, salvage rights, back-yard repair and refurbishment services and marketing. The association's officers, each of whom has an intimate knowledge of the business of their members, are elected from the membership. They have insider information enabling them to assess and implement loans to members with a minimum of fuss and red tape. Consequently, the association has the capacity to mount a microinvestment, business-expansion credit-based income-generation programme of substantial proportions. It also has the ability to monitor and enforce repayment discipline procedures on individual members that neither the co-operating NGO, YIS nor the normal impersonal systems employed by banks can replicate. At the group level there are substantial advantages if the CIGP can be implemented through a formal membership organization. For obvious reasons we call this minimalist sort of group-based programme the umbrella model.

The third model in this group comes closest to acting like a pseudo-banking programme for the poor. It is called the board-driven model because it depends on the existence of an active and committed board of directors for its lending procedures and client-outreach programme. It seems to work best where existing entrepreneurs, who are unable to obtain finance form formal lending institutions, are provided with expansion loans in order to increase the income- and employment-generating capacity of their existing enterprises. The board members are active in assessing the loan proposals received, negotiating with loan applicants, and make an effort to pass on their management skills during the loan-application and repayment-monitoring processes. The model is highly sensitive to the quality of talent available on the board and amongst loan-staff of the programme.

The board-driven model could easily devolve into a bureaucratic top-down programme but it can avoid this danger by involving the community it seeks to assist in the administration and promulgation of its programme. In the Philippines there is a board-driven CIGP, called Tulay Sa Pag-unlad Incorporated (TSPI) which specializes in micro-enterprise expansion loans. It loaned 20,000 pesos, about $800, to a bright young person, let us call him Pacito, who had started an electroplating business. Since that first loan the programme has made a further 130 loans, each less than half the original amount, to help other people enter the same industry on a sub-contract basis, producing electroplated jewellery to order for the original borrower. Each of these persons was introduced to TSPI by Pacito. He not only selected each applicant as a trustworthy borrower but also trained them all into the trade and ensured that they were sufficiently skilled to be competent operators. This has not only created permanent employment for those involved, all of whom had previously had only part-time or itinerant work; it has also provided a role in client selection for the community in a way that made them see TSPI as a programme in which they are more than simple borrowers. It was in Pacito's own interest to see TSPI succeed as this freed him, as the innovating entrepreneur, to concentrate on marketing the goods that are now produced by these many independent and co-operating operators.

In each of these three models the indigenous NGO provides local micro-entrepreneurs access to finance arranged through local fundraising and financial support from a partner NGO or official overseas aid agency. To the foreign partner the collaboration offers local knowledge, the ability to intermediate on behalf of potential borrowers and the capacity to nurture a locally viable mechanism for the development of an on-going financial service to businesses ineligible to secure investment finance from formal lending institutions. The local NGO also has the ability to ensure that the local legal, administrative and documentation standards demanded by the constitutional and accountability constraints that are binding on the foreign partner can be fulfilled.

Savings-linked credit group
The second group of models has as its distinguishing characteristic the mobilization of savings by the client group as an

important component of CIGP investment finance. There are three primary models in the savings-linked credit group, the simplest being RoSCA (revolving savings and credit association model). There are several forms of RoSCA depending upon how the savings and credit rules are crafted. The variety of rules is limited only by the imagination of the organizers, but the choice of which to employ is normally determined by what works in the specific situation confronted by the programme. The basic aim of the RoSCA is the regular provision of working capital on a predictable basis to each RoSCA member. Typically each member is required to save a specific amount on a regular basis. Among the poorest people the RoSCA may define an amount to be saved on a daily or weekly basis; among the less poor the savings period may be as long as a month, but the norm for most programmes is a weekly cycle. On the lending side a complementary set of rules will apply. At the end of each savings period the sum saved is loaned to a member of the RoSCA for use as investment finance. The repayments required are in addition to the regular savings demanded as a member of the association. The borrowing right passes to each person in turn, and the cycle repeats so long as repayments have been maintained at the agreed rate or better. Failure to meet the repayment schedule is penalized by denial of access to the next round of borrowing entitlement. In some RoSCAs borrowing is not done on a cyclical basis but is limited to members able to demonstrate to the association as a whole that they have a viable investment proposal. NGOs have assisted such groups by helping them establish themselves (typically by providing an initial 'revolving deposit' as a non-borrowing RoSCA member) and by supporting the development of appropriate administrative procedures to institutionalize the RoSCA.

The second model in this group is the solidarity-group model, which shares many of the features of a RoSCA but differs in the manner in which it imposes discipline on borrowers within the group. Each group is small, not more than six persons, with possibly hundreds or even thousands of such groups in a larger co-ordinated CIGP programme. The best-known projects of this sort are probably the Grameen Bank in Bangladesh and several of the PISCES (Programme for Investment in the Small Capital Enterprise Sector) supported programmes in Latin America (see Ashe, 1985a;

Fonstad *et al.*, 1982; Fuglesang and Chandler, 1986; Hossain, 1984). The idea here is to combine the power of self-help with the mutual support of peers within each solidarity group. Each group member stands guarantor for every other member. In this way it is the solidarity group of peers that does the assessment of loan proposals, with programme discipline achieved through the aciduous application of the rule that borrowing rights are based on group rather than individual performance. Hence, it is in each member's interests to ensure that the group polices loans and comes to the aid of group members in need of temporary assistance. In most cases the performance criteria imposed on each group cover both savings and loan-repayment records, with members of a group free to decide among themselves how these targets are to be met. Failure to meet an agreed savings and/or loan-repayment schedule results in all members of the group losing access to borrowing privileges. If an individual member fails to keep up, for whatever reason, it is up to the group to make good if those privileges are to be retained. The programmes that utilize the solidarity-group model as the primary NGO activity may or may not have ancillary individual and community development goals unrelated to group members' saving and investment intentions. However, enterprise support through access to credit is the priority of a solidarity-group programme.

The third model in the savings-linked group is the credit-cooperative model. Most developed country citizens will be familiar with credit co-operatives as they were the bridge to formal banking involvement by most lower-income households in those countries' early years of development. Over time the credit co-operative passes from rapid growth into a long period of decline as members are weaned on to the more traditional debtor and depositor roles of the clients of banks and building societies. In many developed economies it is only recently that credeit co-operatives have made something of a come-back.

In developing countries credit co-operatives have been similarly in decline until recently due to the dismal track record they offered members, but there is reason to believe that they might play a more dynamic role in the future. In Bangladesh, Indonesia, Philippines and Sri Lanka credit co-operatives servicing a variety of client mandates are making a come-back of impressive proportions. They are re-examining their membership bond, and expanding into housing and consumer credit in ways that have made them a convenient vehicle for governments to support public programmes in these areas. The credit co-operative, however, seems better suited to the aspirations and needs of the least poor among the poor than the poorest of the poor.

Welfare-oriented credit group
There are also three representative models in the final group identified along the continuum of CIGP models. Though this group often uses minimalist or solidarity techniques to implement its investment credit programme, typically the income- and employment-generation goals of a credit-finance programme are not the principal aims. Credit is merely a component of a wider welfare-focused programme of broad-based community development, an important part of which will often be the stationing of a community worker to act as a resource person and catalyst and to foster development through empowerment and conscientization activities. Training projects in leadership techniques, a local human rights programme and social action designed to achieve greater equality of opportunity or development of counter-vailing power structures are examples of the sorts of activities other than credit associated with these welfare-linked CIGPs.

The change agent posted to work with the target community is a very important person whose role is also described as a community worker, development facilitator or programme assistant. It is the task of these agents to work themselves out of a job by fostering the growth or creation of local capacity to sustain the community-development initiatives sponsored by the programme. A person filling this post may be either a local national or an expatriate, with a strong preference for the former. The position is typically funded by the co-operating developed-country NGO. The activities undertaken by an agent often result in the underwriting of the transaction costs of the credit programme by the foreign NGO partner, despite the fact that the credit programme may not be the most important aspect of the change agent's role as a welfare officer and community worker. For obvious reasons this model is called the community-development model.

The second welfare-linked model is the broker model. It involves the deliberate attempt to put in place mechanisms or procedures that will allow people to achieve access to the formal financial institutions and practices operating in the economy. Typically this involves some form of agreement between the NGO and a local bank by which the NGO absorbs the transaction costs that the bank is not willing to bear for this clientele. The NGO may, for example, facilitate the collection of savings and keep records on behalf of the bank where they are invested. In return the bank may agree to lend against the security of the savings record established, loans again being administered through the auspices of the NGO. The aim is for the NGO to work itself out of a job as a lender by supporting the creation of a reliable savings and loan-repayment record or participants, which is then meant to provide a basis on which the bank can assess the credit-worthiness and loan-repayment capacity of each individual.

Inevitably the broker model is associated with complementary activities intended to facilitate the transition by poor entrepreneurs into the mainstream of modernization and recorded business practice. Such activities are likely to include informal training sessions about banking procedures and practices, formal literacy classes and professional services intended to strengthen business and management skills. The broker model has a tendency to result in top-down paternalism, aiming as it does to 'do something for poor entrepreneurs', rather than change the system to render it more user-friendly. However, there comes a time when the financial needs of small entrepreneurs out-grow the capacity of NGOs, whether indigenous or foreign, to play the role of banker. There is, therefore, likely to be an on-going need for NGO programmes using this model.

The third type of CIGP in this group is the merchant model. It will be recognized by many people as the quintessential welfare-linked do-gooder programme. It finds its *raison d'être* in the belief that poor people need to be protected from themselves and the unscrupulous exploiters of capitalist economies: the poor are vulnerable and need to be protected from themselves because they cannot read and are not familiar with the range of opportunities available in a competitive market place; consequently, they do not seek out discounts or are unable to benefit from special deals, possibly based on volume or turnover, that the programme can negotiate on their behalf. The poor, the argument continues, are unfamiliar with the intricacies of guarantees, warranties and receipts. They do not benefit from the discounts and refunds available for prompt payment or the penalties associated with chronic repayment delinquency. In each of these respects, the argument runs, the interests of the poor need to be dealt with by those with the relevant expertise. The result is a model in which the borrower rarely if ever sees any money; the programme acquires the desired item(s) or services and supplies these in return for an agreed debt and repayment schedule.

There are any number of agricultural co-operatives in developing countries, established to facilitate access by farmers to fertilizers, seeds, breeding stock and marketing services, that are based on the merchant model, and an increasing number of urban-based CIGP programmes use this model too: in Zimbabwe the Zimbabwe Project has supplied enterprising women and men with sewing machines for the making of school uniforms; in India the Bridge Foundation has assisted borrowers wanting to enter the broiler industry; and several countries, notably Indonesia, India and Pakistan, have distributed dairy cows to smallholders. In each case there are good reasons why the merchant model was regarded as appropriate.

The potential economies of scale in agriculture do make the merchant model attractive, but in urban-based typically non-agricultural enterprises, such as food processing, male and female tailoring, hair-dressing, furniture making, handicrafts and retailing the potential benefits are far less obvious and the model appeals more because it is a way of ensuring that the credit extended is used for the purpose stated at the time of loan application. The model is also open to abuse and corruption. There is probably not a country in the world in which a disastrous merchant-model CIGP cannot be cited. Their success is uniquely sensitive to honest administration by programme management. All too often good people have fallen foul of the moral hazard with which the model always seems to present programme principals. Kickbacks from favoured suppliers, commissions for services rendered, excessive transactions costs, outright thievery and hidden charges are only some of the pitfalls that have proved the downfall of what seems to be the majority of merchant-model credit programmes.

Table 2.2 CIGPs visited for this study

Name	Principal location	Model type* used	Loans made** US$ '000	Average loan size US$	Source notes
1. Grameen	Bangladesh	b1, a3	78927	67	(a)
2. TCCS Ltd	Sri Lanka	b3, a3, c1	20107	995	(b)
3. BRAC	Bangladesh	c1, b1, a3	5452	64	(c)
4. KREP	Kenya	a2, a3, c2, c1	4200	1200	(d)
5. WVSL	Sri Lanka	b1, c1, a3	2800	24	(b)
6. PBSP	Philippines	b1, c1, a3	2000	112	(e)
7. CCDB	Bangladesh	c1, a2, b1, a3, c3	1507	41	(f)
8. TSPI	Manila, Philippines	a3, c2	1030	1885	(g)
9. MBM	Bali, Indonesia	a1, c1, c3	760	207	(h)
10. CULB	Bangladesh	b3, a3	742	806	(i)
11. NCCK	Kenya	a3, a1, c2, c1	798	172	(d)
12. PfPK	Kenya	a3, c2	323	807	(d)
13. ZPT	Zimbabwe	a2, c2, a3, c1	224	1048	(j)
14. Caritas	Bangladesh	c1, b1, a1, a3	210	162	(i)
15. KMBI	Valenzuela, Philippines	a3, c1	186	420	(g)
16. DTCL	Nairobi, Kenya	a3, a1, c2	146	4856	(d)
17. JSA	Sri Lanka	a3, a1, c1, c2	128	2100	(b)
18. TBF	India	a3, a1, b2, c3	124	2074	(k)
19. TSKI	Iloilo, Philippines	a3, c3	59	496	(g)
20. ZWB	Zimbabwe	a2, a3, c2, b1	46	136	(k)
21. YIS	Java, Indonesia	c1, b3, a2, c2, a3	35	153	(i)
22. DMCS	Zimbabwe	a1, c1	26	142	(j)
23. DST	India	a1, c3, c2	9	154	(k)
24. VOICE	Zimbabwe	a2, a3, c2	–	170	(j)
25. Oxfam	India	c1	–	–	(l)
26. SLBDC	Sri Lanka	a3, c2	–	–	(l)

* Types of CIGP models. See text (pp. 50–60) for description of each type.

a1. Integrity model	b1. Soladarity-group model	c1. Community-development model
a2. Umbrella model	b2. RoSCA model	c2. Broker model
a3. Board-driven model	b3. Credit-cooperative model	c3. Merchant model

The models used by each programme are shown in order of importance.

** From commencement of programme; some are 10 years old, others only 2 or 3 years.

Notes to sources

(a) Data refer to 1976–87 @ exchange rate of Taka31=US$1. Yunis, 1988 and Mann, Grindle and Shipton, 1989.

(b) Exchange rate of Rp27=US$1 applies. Fernando, 1986; JSA, 1987; IIDI, 1987; Jacobi, 1988; Hutchison, 1984; Wijayapala and Gamage, 1986; Ekanayake and Hettiarachchi, 1986; and personal interviews.

(c) Data refer to 1979–87 @ exchange rate of Taka31=US$1. Leeuen, 1987; Moloney, 1985; BRAC, 1987; and personal interviews.

(d) Exchange rate of Ksh16=US$1. KREP funding covers the period 1984–9. NCCK data refer to the period 1983–7. Ashe, 1985b; Bigelow *et al.*, 1987; KREP, 1985; Hunt and Mirero, 1985; Riungu and Nzioki, 1986; Tripatsas, Crichlow and Gnanakuru, 1987; project documents and personal interviews.

(e) PBSP Annual Reports, various years; de Chavez *et al.*, 1987; Callanta, 1987. The average loan size estimate is based on data from PBSP's Metro Manila Livelihood Programme, 1982–6, which covered 603 loans totalling Peso1.2m, plus Peso16.8m loaned to 7,089 enterprises in 1987–8.

(f) Data refer to 1980–8 @ exchange rate of Taka31=US$1. Primary sources are CCDP Annual Reports, various years; Moloney, 1985; Akhtar, 1988; CCDP Study Team Report, 1987; and personal interviews.

(g) Data refer to 1982–8, supplied by TSPI and published in the Annual Report. An exchange rate of US$=Peso21 has been used in all conversions. Data refer to 1985–8 in the case of KMBI and 1986–8 for TSKI. Both are provincial partner programme of TSPI, and summary data on each are published in the TSPI Annual Report.

(h) Data refer to period 1981–7. Average exchange used US$1=Rp900. Data supplied by MBM.

(i) Data refer to 1979–87 @ exchange rate of Taka31=US$1. Caritas Annual Reports, various years; WCCU, 1987; Moloney, 1985; and personal interviews.

(j) Exchange rate of Z$3.5=US$1; ZPT figures refer to the period 1983–7; DMCS data refer to the period 1985–8; Acton, 1987; Anon, 1988; Else, 1987; Mapondera, 1986; Anon, 1987; private papers and personal interviews.

(k) (j) Exchange rate of Rp13=US$1. Dasgupta, 1987; IIDI, 1987; Annual Reports, various years; and personal interviews.

(l) Both programmes are active in the support of microenterprises in the informal sector, but it was not possible to discover the extent of their financial commitment to CIGPs.

An overview of CIGPs visited

The projects visited during field-work for this study are listed in Table 2.2. There are 26 of them in seven countries. Additional information was gleaned from an extensive review of the literature, including that relating to Central and South America. Overall, the CIGPs visited had an average loan size of around $300, with the median below $100. The most common models encountered were the board-driven, community-development, broker, solidarity and umbrella models.

Observations on programmes visited

It is not my intention in what follows to judge or in some way pretend to evaluate and rank the programmes visited against a predetermined standard. The vignettes offered are presented in order that the reader might better appreciate the import of the data drawn from the experiences of these NGOs. I trust that the observations made do not understate the valuable work that is being done and the pioneering role that NGOs have played in the conduct of CIGPs established in partnership with the poor of the Third World.

The order in which the comments that follow are presented is that in which the countries were visited. It is in no way intended to be a reflection or statement on a rank order by importance, quality or any other measure of performance.

MBM: Maha Bhoga Marga (Way of Prosperity)

This is an independent development foundation based in Bali, Indonesia. Established in 1980, it is an arm of the development programme of the Bali Protestant Church. Its genesis owes much to concern by the hierarchy of the church that its clergy should not be a total burden on parishioners who are, in the main, poor and often amongst the poorest. The success of CIGPs among the clergy was soon extended to the fellowship and then to the community as a whole. Today MBM has more extant loans to non-church members than it has to members and CIGP activities account for more than half total annual expenditures. Foreign NGO support has come from IIDI (the Institute for International Development Inc., now known as Opportunity International), EZE, Maranatha Trust and other bilateral aid sources.

A comprehensive review of MBM's CIGP programme was completed for USAID in 1987 by Mary Judd and David Bussau. This study was based on interviews and an in-depth analysis of more than a quarter of MBM's three and a half thousand loans for small-enterprise development. The indicators of success that they recorded are:

○ on-time repayment rate averages between 80 and 90 per cent per annum, with the balance informally rescheduled
○ the bad debt or default record in the seven years of the programme's operation has averaged less than one-half of one per cent
○ market rates of interest are charged, averaging 25 per cent per annum, plus one-off fees of 2.5 per cent of the loan amount to cover transactions cost
○ the average repayment period per loan is less than six months
○ a quarter of the loans made are micro loans, that is, less than Rp50,000, another quarter are small, less than Rp100,000, and the third quarter are medium size, Rp100,000–200,000. The average loan size over the period 1981–6 was Rp162,889 (approx. US$110)
○ on average one sustained wage-earning job was created for every 5 loans made, that is, an investment of Rp815,000 (approx. US$550) per job, not counting increased use of family labour not paid a cash wage or the employment of the borrower

○ annual growth rate of loans disbursed has averaged more than 125 per cent; and

○ four-fifths of the loans have been made to female borrowers.

MBM is primarily a personal integrity model programme, relying on the recommendation of trusted persons, such as the local pastor, a village leader or a well-known and respected programme participant, to select persons to whom loans are to be made. The MBM board, which has legal responsibility for MBM, does not get involved in programme administration or loan approvals unless a very large, that is in excess of Rp1m = approx. US$650, loan request is being considered. The board is also responsible for MBM policy although there is a tendency to defer to the wishes of the hierarchy of the Bali Protestant Church.

Repayment procedures used by MBM are tailored to the needs and constraints on individual borrowers. In a very poor district, such as Singaraja in the north of Bali, daily repayment procedures are followed, but at Kapal, the headquarters region near Denpasar, where the standard of living tends to be higher and average loan size more than twice as high, weekly and monthly repayment arrangements are used. A savings-link had also been introduced in Singaraja in an effort to increase loanable funds, promote regional self-reliance and as a means of ensuring that borrowing requests are tied, in at least a loose way, to the ability to repay. Prospective borrowers must save with the programme for not less than a month prior to becoming eligible to borrow. The Singaraja programme claims to have dispersed Rp56m to 1987, with an estimated 685 jobs created and virtually no defaulting borrowers despite 31 business failures out of 369 loans made. 83 per cent of loans were for merchandizing investments, a figure common to the MBM programme overall.

YIS: Yayasan Indonesia Sejahtera (Indonesian Welfare Foundation)

The headquarters for YIS are at Solo, a famous tourist destination and centre of batik production in Central Java, north from Jogjakata. Established in 1974, it evolved from a health-oriented programme led by an ecumenical group of lay people and developed a style all its own based on group participation. It has a strong training component designed to prepare village workers and change agents. The creation and nurturing of coherent groups is a key part of what YIS does. Consequently, its style betrays it as a welfare first community-development model, which uses the credit-co-operative and umbrella models as primary mechanisms for distributing its financial support for CIGPs. Its involvement in village-level CIGPs did not begin until 1983.

At the beginning of 1988 YIS was actively supporting CIGPs operated by 228 co-operating groups, with each group not smaller than 25 persons and the largest more than 150 strong. YIS lending is always to the group, with the group left to define its own on-lending policies and procedures. The bias in group memberships favours women, especially in the smaller village credit groups.

In order to ensure that the group strategy works effectively YIS devotes considerable effort to training group leaders and works with these leaders to define group savings targets, capital needs and other areas of YIS/group collaboration. These training activities are increasingly provided on a cost-plus basis, and the demand is now so great that training is a major source of locally generated revenue for YIS. Foreign support has come primarily from the West German NGO, Evangelische Zentralstelle fur Entwicklungshifte (EZE).

Once the group has achieved its savings target it becomes eligible for a YIS seeding loan of Rp250,000, which is provided to the group using the broker model. The group is introduced to a local bank and repayments are made by regular deposits in a loan-repayment account. The intention here is to establish for the group and eventually individual members a track record that can be used as a basis for access to bank loans. Once repayments reach 75 per cent of the principal and interest, the group is eligible for another YIS loan, the size of which is open to negotiation. YIS loans to the group can be repaid in not more than two years, but it is in the interest of each group to repay as soon as it can if it wants a repeat loan of a larger amount. On-lending by groups is for durations that vary widely, but average duration quoted by groups visited clustered around 11–12 weeks.

YIS has encountered problems with its broker model. At both the local village and the district levels bank officials are impressed with the savings and loan-repayment track record established by the groups (most are co-operatives of one sort or another) and are keen to enter the market to capture a share of the profits they can see are to be made from lending to the poor. Alas, the provincial and headquarters authorities of the co-operating banks have been unwilling to waive extant collateral and other policies that prevent the YIS groups and their members from accessing regular bank loans. This frustrating experience is common to every CIGP programme visited that has sought to play the broker on behalf of its clients. But YIS is persisting and in 1988 launched a pilot programme with Bank Rakyat Indonesia, with funding of around US$1m over three years from EZE and the government of the Federal Republic of Germany, to link both saving to credit and formal sector banks to informal sector self-help groups in Indonesia.

YIS loans are small by any standards. The initial seeding loan per group is only Rp250,000 (US$170 or US$5.50 per person for a group of 30 members). This money is loaned by YIS at 1.5 per cent per month, reducing, but the groups typically on-lend to their members at three or four times this rate. At this rate there is excess demand as the village moneylender rate is typically 10–30 per cent per month, depending upon the season and the purpose for which the loan is sought. Group financial capacity to lend is, therefore, strongly dependent on the success of the group savings programme, the results of which are added to the pool for recycling as loans to group members. Savings targets per person per group vary widely but the range quoted was Rp5,000–15,000 per month.

YIS-supported groups have some impressive performance indicators. The on-time repayment rate is 99 per cent, with no defaults. The four groups visited indicated increases in income as a result of the programme that averaged 100 per cent over twelve months, but this was from a pitifully low level of earnings of only Rp500–1000 per day. This is indicative of the poor state in which participants had existed and continue to exist despite their success. The fact that many of the programme beneficiaries are women who previously were among the vulnerable poor makes these data more explicable but also serves to underline the critical contribution that such programmes can and do make to poverty alleviation.

The essence of the group loan process is that each group is expected to collectively cover the cost of defaults or repayment delays by individual members. In this respect the YIS model also has a flavour of the solidarity model about it. YIS also has a highly charismatic leader, whom staff and clients defer to as 'Patrisno' or 'father', and an active and committed board of lay persons drawn from all the major denominations in Indonesia — the current board president is a Moslem; his predecessor was a Catholic. YIS, therefore, also shares qualities of the board-driven model.

TSPI: Tulay Sa Pag-unlad. Inc. (Bridge to Progress) and its provincial partners, KMBI and TKSI

This Philippines NGO is the product of collaboration between a group of Filipino and American Christian business people. It began operations in 1982 and has proved itself such a winner in the field of CIGP programmes that it is in progress of replicating itself by nurturing the development of independent sister programmes in each province of the Philippines. KMBI and TSKI are only two of the six that had been launched by the end of June 1988.

TSPI and its sister programmes KMBI and TSKI are examples of a board-driven model. The boards of these programmes are active not only in policy formulation and fundraising but also in the client selection and loan-programme monitoring procedures used to implement the CIGP. Board members are also in the vanguard as lobbyists on behalf of programme beneficiaries to get as many participants as possible promoted from the 'non-bankable' to 'bankable' category. In this respect the broker model applies but so does the personal integrity model as references from one's priest or pastor are the first filter through which eligible borrowers must pass. The referee is required to complete a detailed questionnaire on the potential borrower.

TSPI specializes in expansion loans to existing enterprises rather than support for aspiring entrepreneurs. This is less true of KMBI and TSKI, in part because the level of poverty in the rural provinces and the slum districts beyond Manila proper is worse, the lack of investment finance more pervasive and demand from aspiring entrepreneurs more easily identified. TSPI operates primarily in the top three tiers of the Poverty Pyramid, while the provincial programmes make many more very small loans to borrowers from amongst the vulnerable poor, especially women. Nonetheless, as a matter of philosophy all the programmes in the TSPI family have a bias in favour of expansion loans to microenterprises that are going concerns. It is felt that this strategy allows for the implementation of a simpler programme with less need to assess the business or the proposal for which the investment loan is being sought. The fact that the borrower is already a successful micro-entrepreneur and is vouched-for as a trust-worthy person by the local clergy is regarded as sufficient collateral.

TSPI and its provincial replicates make individual loans and do not normally incorporate a savings link into their lending activities. Repayments are tailored to individual needs and programme staff, in concert with members of the board, take primary responsibility for assessing project proposals, monitoring loan repayments and nurturing client involvement in programme expansion. Selection of able and committed staff and board representation is, of course, critical to programme performance.

In order to contain the burden of transaction costs, TSPI has imposed a minimum loan size on its lending (this does not apply to the provincial partners). In 1988 the limit was Peso10,000 (US$500). In addition repayment procedures were streamlined and responsibility for seeing that funds are available to service the loan placed back on the borrower. To achieve this TSPI uses a post-dated cheque system, whereby post-dated cheques are signed at the time the loan is made to the client, and these are then presented at the bank by TSPI on a regular, normally monthly, basis for drawing against a deposit account established in the name of the borrower for this purpose. The borrower undertakes to make regular deposits in amounts not less than are necessary to meet the agreed repayment schedule. In time it is hoped that clients and their projects should become bankable. Early in 1988 TSPI entered into negotiations with the Bank of Philippines Foundation to enhance this brokering role by experimenting with alternative ways in which the credit needs of small borrowers could be serviced without blowing out overhead and administration costs.

The average loan size for TSPI is relatively large for a CIGP and belies the large number of small loans that are made. Not less than a quarter of all loans fall in the US$500–700 range. However, the emphasis on expansion loans means that TSPI, KMBI, TSKI and the other provincial sister programmes rely on their capacity to generate jobs to help the poor in the lowest levels of the Poverty Pyramid. At this task they have established an impressive record having created, on average, a sustained wage-paying job for every US$380 loaned. A job created is defined as employment paying a minimum of Peso54 a day, five days per week. If one adds the impact of these loans on part-time wage employment, self-employment and utilization of family labour, the employment spin-off may well total to the equivalent of more than 4,000 jobs for an overall investment in income-generation project loans of only marginally more than US$1m over six years.

TSPI is unique not only because it has a replication programme in full swing but also because it has adopted a 'viability model' as an operating and management strategy. The essence of this board-led policy is to nurture an independence of TSPI and the provincial programmes from their current dependence on the financial support of sponsoring NGOs and official aid contributions within six years. A cornerstone of this strategy is a loan interest-rate policy that seeks equality with the going commercial rate in the formal banking sector (currently 26 per cent a year effective), cost recovery for consultancy services provided to clients, a spread in the loan portfolio across a broad range of loan sizes to contain programme exposure to risk and vigorous local fund-raising efforts.

PBSP: Philippines Business for Social Progress

This organization is an example of the umbrella model, set up in December 1970 as a response by the Philippines Council for Economic Development, the Philippines Business Council and the Philippines Association for Social Action to the social unrest and economic downturn that characterized that year in the Philippines. Based on a Venezuelan programme of corporate social action, PBSP was a means by which the Philippines business community could rationalize and co-ordinate its funding and technical support to socio-economic projects and programmes across the country.

Although PBSP is a corporate programme it is essentially community-group focused using the community-development model to reach its clients. It has a primary commitment to fostering the establishment and improvement of local community organizations, such as various sorts of co-operatives, marketing groups, village-level NGOs involved in delivery of community services, education bodies and local

71

professional and civic groups. PBSP's CIGP involvement is, therefore, largely one implemented at arms length through loans and grants to such organizations for CIGP purposes. PBSP also sees itself as being able to play an important part in poverty alleviation in the Philippines as a broker between micro-entrepreneurs in poverty and those domestic and foreign agencies in the formal modern economy that have resources currently denied the poor for one reason or another. In both the brokering role and as a direct lender to community-based groups, PBSP channels resources that are on-lent for income-generation purposes. Between 1971 and 1987 an estimated US$2m was channelled to CIGPs, which is approximately one-quarter of PBSP's total income for this period.

Ultimately PBSP sees itself as a foundation dedicated to the establishment of community-based credit extension structures that will enable the poor, who do not usually have access to formal credit sources, to improve their livelihood prospects. These extension activities include CIGPs plus a range of training, expert consulting services and administrative supports designed to improve the prospects of successfully establishing institutions and community structures that can ensure the viable continuation of the programme after PBSP is no longer involved. PBSP hopes that this grassroots strategy will, in the three years 1988–91, result in the creation of 1,800 new full-time jobs, 150,000 self-reliant households and the organization of 15 provincial federations of poverty groups in the Filipino community.

PBSP has the distinction of being a self-reliant indigenous NGO. Its major sources of income are contributions from member companies (67 per cent) and interest income from funds loaned to PBSP's poverty programme (28 per cent). Each of its 118 member companies contributes 0.6 per cent of pre-tax income as its share of PBSP annual income, which in 1987–8 amounted to Peso74.8m (US$3.6m).

CCDB: Christian Commission for Development in Bangladesh
This is a savings-linked solidarity group model which also uses the umbrella and the community-development models to implement its programme. CCDB is a service organization of the National Christian Council of Bangladesh, covering nine programme areas; CIGPs are one of the nine. Credit is a

component in the multisectoral approach operated by CCDB, the overall goal being the creation of communities characterized by self-reliance and distributive justice. In this holistic approach to development, credit is not necessarily regarded as any more or any less important than skills training, development, education, primary health-care or some other component of the multisectoral strategy of 'people upliftment'.

The CCDB credit programme is also a community-training activity, designed to use peer pressure to reinforce the notion that credit taken confers a responsibility on the borrower to repay the loan with interest and prescribed service charges. Savings are inherent to the programme and no loans are made to persons who do not demonstrate the discipline essential to this activity. All savings are handled via a local bank in an effort to establish for clients an official bank track record. Repeat loans are made a function of the credit worthiness established as a programme participant in both the savings and the debt-repayment areas. The savings component has become the backbone of the revolving fund that sets the limit on total finance available for lending. Of the Taka9.4m loaned in 1987–8, Taka8.8m came from repayments received from existing borrowers. The balance is new money injected from the contributions of foreign-based partner NGOs. In CCDB's case the most important of these in terms of financial contributions are WCC, AFFHC, BfdW and EZE (see Acronyms). Only 35 per cent of CCDB's programme is devoted to the provision of credit.

Group membership is essential to the operation of this welfare-linked CIGP. At the beginning of February 1988, it had 2,400 small groups participating, with a total of 17,300 beneficiaries. Group size varied between 5 and 9 persons. CCDB loans are made to the groups as either small loans of not more than Taka1,500 for a maximum six months duration, or medium loans of not more than Taka3,500 for a maximum twelve months duration. The group can then on-lend to members of not less than five months good standing within the group. The group is responsible to CCDB for the loans made to each individual, but CCDB will reschedule where loan delinquency arises from causes beyond the control of the borrower and the group. In a country plagued by natural disasters, especially the annual floods, this is regarded as essential. Nonetheless, debt rescheduling is a step taken reluctantly and only after the concurrence of the debtor's peers. Legal steps for recovery of debt from defaulters are rigorously pursued where the debtor clearly has the capacity to repay but refuses to accept the legal responsibility that flows from the advance by CCDB to the solidarity group.

CCDB repayment mechanisms are negotiated according to the circumstances of each group, but it is a hard and fast rule that procedures regarding when, where, by whom, how much and how frequently must be clearly spelled out from the outset. Typically the solidarity-group leader is in charge of collecting repayments from individual members, and the amount due from the group as a whole is handed to the CCDB community worker at a regular group meeting. The group may meet as frequently as weekly to discuss matters that members may wish to raise. Often these are business concerns on which individuals seek advice from their peers in the group (it is intended that groups should consist of persons from similar backgrounds and occupation). Repayments to CCDB by the solidarity group may only be quarterly, but for individuals in the group repayments are typically set at more frequent intervals, sometimes as often as daily, depending upon the group's assessment of what is needed to ensure repayments are on time and not less than the scheduled amount.

The greater part of CCDB's client group is in rural areas well beyond the urban centres such as those around Dhaka. There are important consequences of this rural focus, the most significant being the exposure of the programme to the vagaries of weather and flood damage which are perennial problems facing farmers in Bangladesh. CCDB tends, therefore, to have a higher proportion of agriculture-related investment loans, including microenterprises in fisheries, livestock, irrigation and tube-well projects. Consequently, the number of occasions when groups are faced with having to default or seek a rescheduling of loans for reasons beyond their control is higher (up to 15 per cent of medium-size loans have had to be written off in recent years following severe flooding that not only inundated villages, fields and fish ponds but slashed available feed sources for surviving livestock). The CCDB experience in this regard reinforces the general observation that CIGPs are not so well suited to

the financial needs of agricultural-production microenterprises, the fortunes of which are subject to significant risks
over which the borrower has little or no control. The vagaries
of weather expose agricultural enterprises to risks with which
non-farm wage-goods microenterprises do not have to contend. The risks of doing business in the latter are not so great
as to render the entire solidarity group vulnerable to failure
from a common cause. Smallholder agricultural production
needs a different sort of credit programme with far more
extensive financial backing than is possible from the reserves
of a solidarity group or an entire NGO-directed CIGP.

Another implication of the rural bias in the CCDB programme is that the proportion of loans going to women is
lower than in similar programmes concentrated in the major
urban centres. Sixty per cent of CCDB beneficiaries are
women. However, the smallest loans continue to be made
primarily to women and the on-time repayment rate for their
very small loans remains at an impressively high 97 per cent.

BRAC: Bangladesh Rural Advancement Committee

As with most major NGOs in Bangladesh, BRAC finds its
origins in the relief and rehabilitation required following the
war of liberation. Since 1972, BRAC has expanded its horizons to encompass poverty alleviation as the key to equitable
development. Its Rural Credit and Training Programme, begun in 1979, is central to this strategy.

BRAC has grown into a quintessential example of the
modern community-development model. Like CCDB,
BRAC's investment-loans policy employs the discipline of
the solidarity-group model. It has adopted this policy for a
number of reasons, the most important of which are:

○ group-based loans are simpler to keep on a high on-time
  repayment footing
○ individual savings targets are easier to encourage and
  monitor when conducted in groups; and
○ BRAC believes that groups are a more effective means to
  institutionalizing its welfare activities, which are dedicated
  to 'value revision' and 'value formation' in an effort to
  overcome the fatalism with which the poor in Bangladesh
  are afflicted.

BRAC's CIGP groups consist, on average, of five like-
minded people. The group must meet regularly in order to

report and share individual progress, facilitate loan-repayment collections and provide a reliable contact point with BRAC's programme organizers, any one of whom is responsible for not more than 10 villages. In each village there are not likely to be more than 20 CIGP groups, 10 for the men and 10 for the women.

In January 1986 BRAC launched its current CIGP which it calls its Rural Development Programme. In the eighteen months to June 1987 it had taken this programme to 1,523 villages and serviced 141,645 persons with an average investment loan of US$29. All loans are made through the village based groups, to which BRAC lends at a competitive 18 per cent simple. The groups on-lend to members at a premium of 3 to 4 per cent. The results show 51 per cent of these borrowers were women and the on-time repayment rate was 91 per cent. Overall, however, taking all BRAC lending for CIGP purposes since its inception into account, 61 per cent of BRAC loans have gone to men and 39 per cent to women, but the on-time repayment rate remains above 90 per cent.

Fifty-six per cent of BRAC loans are short-term, less than 12 months, 37 per cent for terms of up to three years and the remainder are long term. This is consistent with a programme that lends for production rather than trading activities. Only 32 per cent of BRAC-financed micro-enterprises are in the trading sector, while agricultural production, animal husbandry and fish culture account for 37 per cent and food processing for another 17.5 per cent.

In 1986 BRAC added to its CIGP strategy a Rural Enterprise Programme (REP), the need for which was seen to come from the distortion in felt needs that living at the margin of survival generates. The vulnerable and labouring poor often find it difficult to see a way out of the misery that has become their accustomed lot. In order to lift them beyond this level and ensure that they do not fall foul of the 'copy-cat-syndrome', that is do what someone else has done, the rural enterprise project seeks to identify areas of enterprise and economic opportunity that offer a better prospect for livelihood than labouring, piecework or begging. BRAC has found that there are now many microenterprise areas that are so intensively served that competition makes it hard for new entrants to rise above survival earnings (estimated at Taka500 a month). REP is an experiment in opportunity identification and assessment that marks the BRAC out from

Agricultural supplies are the core of merchant-model schemes. India

Making bricks by hand – they are later fired and hardened

among those programmes that specialize in expansion loans for existing activities or finance for enterprises that solidarity-group members are willing to back with their status as loan guarantors.

One of BRAC's most successful endeavours has been the link that it insists must exist between its lending for productive purposes and savings. By April 1988 total savings by rural groups had topped Taka30m, which is about half the size of the revolving fund from which credits are extended by BRAC to approved borrowers. BRAC's dilemma is to find a more effective use for these funds. Currently they are held on deposit with local banks in what is so far a vain hope that the banks will, in turn, begin to lend to individuals or groups from which these deposits come. The local banks continue to accept BRAC deposits and follow their traditional strategy of lending rural deposits to urban formal-sector borrowers.

Grameen Bank, Bangladesh

This is a CIGP that is so successful that it has developed from the status of an NGO to that of a unique bank serving exclusively the investment needs of the landless poorest of the poor, that is, the vulnerable and labouring poor. It began as an experiment in rural development under the leadership of the Professor of Economics at Chittagong University, Professor Muhammad Yunus. Initial funding came from the Ford Foundation, the Janata Bank and the Bangladesh National Agricultural Bank. The first loans were made in 1976. Several years of struggle ensued before Grameen had developed sufficiently to take on the title bank in 1983. It is now a joint-stock company with 75 per cent of shares owned by the landless borrowers who are its clients and the remaining 25 per cent owned by the government of Bangladesh. Progress since then is summarized by Professor Yunus:

> Today (1988) it has 400,000 borrowers, 82 per cent of whom are women. Grameen Bank lends out more than US$2.5m each month in tiny loans averaging US$67. Its recovery rate is 98 per cent. Now it has over 400 branches working in 8,000 villages (out of 68,000) in Bangladesh. Borrowers have accumulated over US$7.0m in their savings funds. (1988:2)

Grameen Bank operates as a savings-linked model of the solidarity-group type, with an active policy-making board of directors taken from among its borrowers. It shares, therefore, some characteristics of the board-driven model. It also has institution-building aspects in the way it runs its group-formation and bank-operating procedures that also allow it to be classed in the community-development mold.

All lending by Grameen is done through its groups of land-less poor. Each group consists of five persons, each of whom shares a common socio-economic situation and similar aspirations. Each group must be reasonably homogeneous in its occupational membership; this improves the stock of accumulated knowledge that the group can call upon when assessing loan requests from its members. Moreover, a group has to meet specified criteria before it is accepted into the Grameen circle, which is done with considerable ceremony to mark the event as a significant achievement. These criteria include the attainment of savings goals, a group meeting track record which demonstrates the commitment of each member to the group, plus evidence of a sustainable capacity for the group to meet regularly for the mutual support of members. In other words, the group must demonstrate a degree of cohesion, a commitment to mutual support, and a capacity for rigorous integrity in assessing one another's schemes that mark the members out as having formed a viable solidarity group.

Trust in people is a critical part of the Grameen philosophy. Trust requires reliance on people's integrity and acceptance that the poor are not sub-human; it is the conditions in which the poor are forced to live that are sub-human. Consequently, Grameen relies on its solidarity groups explicitly, and puts the responsibility back onto the group to assess loan proposals and impose Grameen financial procedures. It is the group that is also responsible for ensuring that loans are repaid. Delinquency or default is penalized by denying access to further credit to all members of the group until the problem is rectified or mutually resolved.

The spread of Grameen loans by activity reflects the bias that the bank has towards women as its main target group. More than two-thirds of its loans are for investment in vendor-operated microenterprises, especially petty trading or shopkeeping, plus processing and manufacturing activities that utilize craft and homemaker skills learnt in the household. Agricultural production accounts for less than 5 per cent of Grameen Bank loans.

Interest-rate policy of the Grameen Bank is set by its board, which has directed that in addition to parity with rates offered to borrowers able to qualify for formal-sector bank loans, borrowers must become regular savers plus accept a premium on the advertised interest rate, typically 2–4 per cent. The purpose of the premium is to cover the costs of operating a loan-guarantee fund, make provision for a group-based contribution to an education fund and to support a solidarity-group savings fund. The Grameen approach to investment finance rejects the notion that the poor must receive subsidized loans if they are to succeed. As a bank the Grameen offers its members not only access to bank finance but also a savings deposit institution that recycles these funds into the economy in which they were generated.

Caritas and the Credit Union League of Bangladesh (CULB)
These two organizations work in parallel in Bangladesh. Caritas, the relief and development organization of the Catholic Church, is largely welfare oriented, but rejects the notion that development in Bangladesh requires the input of an increasing flow of foreign resources. For a decade and a half the resource-input strategy has characterized development programming and official policy at the macroeconomic level in Bangladesh, without apparent success as far as poverty is concerned. In 1971 one-fifth of the adult population in Bangladesh was landless; by 1987 this proportion had more than doubled to 55 per cent.

Caritas operates on the principle that it is not resources that count, but resourcefulness. The Caritas revolving fund is small compared to the tens of millions put into rural loans by the Catholic Church prior to 1979 but the directors are confident that their grassroots approach is sufficiently effective to make up the difference. The new strategy is designed to move away from the welfare and relief tag the Church's activities earned before 1979. The new strategy is one that operates through a CIGP programme that stresses 'learning to earn' as a central platform in its efforts to defend the human rights of the landless poor. Consequently, Caritas is not a minimalist credit programme, but one that complements credit with a range of supporting activities that inform clients of their rights as citizens, instruct and assist the poor on how to access government services, especially agricultural extension expertise, and provide basic literacy and numeracy skills training.

Caritas operates on a savings-linked basis through solidarity groups of 15 persons a group. It is intended that these groups will develop into credit unions able to join the CULB family. Caritas requires its member groups to work and save together for twelve months before becoming eligible for a group loan from the Caritas revolving fund. On-lending within the group is limited to 50 per cent of the required investment per project proposal, except in the case of the poorest people, where the savings target is set at 10 per cent of the funding needed for the proposed enterprise. It is the group, however, that is responsible for the repayment of the loan and members are expected to come to the assistance of fellow group members who are experiencing problems meeting their commitments. This seems to work well in so far as the loan default rate is close enough to zero, despite an on-time repayment rate that is below (83v + 90 per cent) that achieved by Grameen, BRAC, CCDB and other similar CIGBs in Bangladesh.

CULB is an outgrowth of dissatisfaction among its founders, including Caritas, with the farce that the traditional co-operative system in Bangladesh had become. Caritas in particular found it impossible to work with institutions that insisted on kick-backs, produced books that matched whatever recipe was called for by the occasion and were slowly being bled dry by the practice of extending loans for the repayment of earlier loans in order to keep their performance records in the black.

Since its founding in 1979, CULB has grown to an organization of 23,000 members in 30 credit unions. Only 4,500 of these members, that is, two credit unions, are in urban areas. Savings and the use of member savings for the benefit of members is crucial to the credit-union model. Loans are based on demonstrated capacity to save, with an upper limit to loans to members of ten times funds on deposit. CULB member credit unions will lend for consumption purposes but there is a strong preference for loan applications that are investment oriented because of a subsidiary concern to see the rate of job creation for the poor increased in Bangladesh. Overall CULB members have an on-time repayment rate of 98 per cent. They also tend to be better off and in the upper levels of the Poverty Pyramid, having graduated from the depths of poverty at which Caritas finds its primary focus of activity.

WVSL: World Vision Sri Lanka

This CIGP is unique for a number of reasons, not least because, despite its spectacular success, it is no longer supported at an official level by the foreign-sponsoring NGO, World Vision International, which had been instrumental in getting it off the ground. The decision to discontinue sponsorship is in part a response to success; WVSL's CIGP must rank as one of the most successful programmes anywhere in the world. Its success has enabled it to develop a life of its own that is no longer dependent upon continued nurturing activity by the foreign sponsor. However, the decision has also severely limited the local programme's capacity to replicate itself and fulfil its potential as a major poverty alleviation initiative on the national scale in Sri Lanka. Nonetheless, one can understand WVI's decision to pull back as a rational response by an international NGO to depart an area of Third World development in which it had not previously had great joy anywhere in the world. In place of the CIGP programme, WVSL has returned its concentration to the child sponsorship field, where its partner, WVI, does have a demonstrated comparative advantage worldwide.

The hallmarks of the WVSL credit programme can be stated as follows:

○ First, it was based on close co-operation with existing social and institutional structures to monitor implementation procedures and access expert technical assistance from official government sources. The programme deliberately sought to use the infrastructure and the bureaucracy already in place rather than develop its own support systems and interface with domestic local government and planning authorities.
○ Second, the programme was village based with all members of a co-operating village able to participate so long as specified individual savings targets were met.
○ Third, the programme was run entirely by village personnel, with such things as loan application assessments, loan administration and collection procedures entirely the responsibility of the village and its elected CIGP administrators. Representatives from government agencies on the

CIGP committee are there in a non-voting capacity as observers, resource persons and advisers.

○ Fourth, programme discipline and protection against the corrosive force of corruption is seated not in organizational procedures but in the requirement that the village hold regular open meetings to announce successful loan applicants, record repayments received, discuss delinquencies and allow comment on how village savings can be utilized to complement the goals sought of the CIGP programme. Openness of all programme details regularly and formally broadcast was the mechanism chosen by the programme's founder and designer to mobilize community enthusiasm, encourage broad participation and harness the discipline of peer review and peer pressure.

The founder of this Sri Lankan CIGP was the then Director of WVSL, B. Fernando. A local person, he had come to WV as the former Commissioner for Internal Revenue in Sri Lanka. In this position he had learnt a lot about people and the money problems of the poor. He was convinced that a successful CIGP in Sri Lanka demanded trust in the capacity of the people whom the programme was meant to benefit to see success as in their own self-interest. Participants have to see and accept that default is not an option that is open to them if the programme is to achieve its aims. To get to this point may take months of patient work by a project officer resident in the region but not necessarily in the village in question. It is the officer's role to challenge the villagers to express their needs and goals, to assess their own capacity to help one another and themselves and to work with freely elected village leaders to ensure that they can take their place as technically competent and responsible programme administrators. This may require the introduction of a basic literacy and numeracy programme, some training in recordkeeping and assistance in the design of open meetings at which savings and loan targets are announced, debated and publicly recorded.

When the village structures are in place and a modest savings-based revolving fund is in operation, WVSL makes available a once-off grant to the community's revolving fund. The typical grant is US$4,000, and it is this money that forms the core of the CIGP and against which loans to village members are drawn. The size of the fund increases as profits and member savings are ploughed back into the programme. Commercial rates of interest are charged and all profits have been ploughed back into the fund in all cases, though it is open to the village to have the fund waste away if this is their decision. In the ten years up to when WVI withdrew in 1987, not one of the 700 villages to which the programme had been taken had decided to waste their revolving fund. On the contrary, overall these 700 village funds have experienced a 98 per cent on-time repayment rate, compared to less than 40 per cent by banks operating in the same geographic areas, and the Colombo office of WVSL is not aware of a single village fund that has disbanded or failed to continue operating successfully. With the departure of WVI as a sponsor, however, there has had to be a halt to the expansion of the programme to new villages.

From the foregoing it is clear that this CIGP shares charateristics of several of the models outlined on pp. 52–62. It is involved in community development, but it is also a savings-linked solidarity group. It differs as a group programme, however, in that the group through which it works is as large as the village in which it is being implemented. In this sense it resembles the umbrella model, with the whole membership able to benefit from loans financed essentially by the village grant from WVI. The average is a community of 100 families, each with an average of 5 members per family. The elected CIGP committee that overseas the implementation and openness procedures numbers 13 persons, including the local Rural Development Officer of the Government of Sri Lanka and the WVSL village worker. The latter two, however, have no official role other than as obsevers and as the persons who are responsible to ensure that the accounts of the village CIGP are independently audited once a year. All other members are elected for a term of nine months, during which time they or their families are ineligible for a programme loan.

Loan delinquency and default have not proven to be a problem for this CIGP. Both are dealt with at the village level, with peer pressure the critical weapon used to maintain individual fiscal discipline. Nonetheless, the model does not reject the importance of corporate responsibility and community support to individual borrowers, especially where business problems or the failure of a microenterprise are clearly attributable to factors beyond the control of the borrower. For example, a loan was given to a widow to begin a small broiler enterprise. She borrowed enough to purchase 50 day-old chicks plus feed to get them started. It transpired that all but one of the chicks were male! She appealed to the CIGP administrators for loan relief. The village meeting decided that the borrower was still liable for the loan but that a period of grace was warranted. In addition, the broiler enterprise was still assessed as sufficiently viable to justify a second loan, provided that the expertise could be secured to ensure against a repetition of the original experience. At the time of my visit the widow was well established in the broiler business, raising village chickens for consumption by buyers who are also her neighbours and fellow CIGP participants.

JSA: Jeeva Sanvardhanaya Ayathanaya
JSA had been operating less than three years when we visited, but had had the benefit of the experience of sister programmes of the Institute for International Development Inc. (IIDI) in South-East Asia, Latin America and Africa. Consequently, in a relatively short period of time JSA had dispensed more than 80 loans from its revolving loan fund at an average amount of US$2,100.

Like TSPI, its sister programme in the Philippines, JSA operates on a philosophy that favours the funding of expansion loans to existing micro-entrepreneurs. This explains, in part, the relatively large average loan size. Loan size at JSA is also influenced by board policy that seeks to minimize programme risk by spreading programme loans across the spectrum of loan sizes. Only 40 per cent of loans were to be given to borrowers seeking less than US$1,000, a further 25 per cent to those seeking less than US$5,000 and the balance to larger loans.

Sri Lanka is a difficult environment in which to work. The security problems and the discombobulation that has accompanied the racial strife between Tamils and Singhalese have sent many a good business to the wall. However, the JSA experience provides at least prima facie evidence that 'it pays to bank on the poor.' In contrast to the performance of WVSL and the TCCS credit programmes, JSA had an on-time repayment rate of only 38 per cent at the time visited. Moreover, of the 23 projects that were a month or more delinquent as at 1 January 1988, only three were in the 'less than US$1,000' category! As a board-driven model, responsibility for this relatively unimpressive record remains with the board and JSA staff rather than the borrowers, but this fact was still to be addressed at the time of my most informative and memorable visit.

It is my understanding that substantial changes have recently been made at the board, staff and policy levels in an attempt to resolve JSA's problems. The results are encouraging. At the end of October 1989, the on-time repayment rate of loans had recovered to exceed 80 per cent.

TBF: The Bridge Foundation, Bangalore, India

Some programmes work in a difficult environment because of the depth of poverty that grips their clients, others because of the area in which they work. TBF's is difficult not only because poverty is so endemic in India, but also because the bureaucratic and legal environment is so complex and restrictive. This bears directly on the sort of 'not-for-profit' self-help endeavours that TBF seeks to foster. In India it is permissible to give charity, but for a community-development agency to suggest that it also wants to make a profit in order to expand its capacity to finance the poor, then the weight of the Indian bureaucracy feels invited to descend upon you. TBF has, therefore, had to develop innovative ways to do its CIGP work. This has included the granting of loans to existing enterprises able to plough-back profits into skills training, loans to local welfare organizations, such as Divya Shanti Trust, and the support of selected clients willing to enter an enterprise in which TBF has a capacity to provide technical assistance and expert advice as well as finance.

TBF is very much a board-driven model operating on the personal integrity principle. TBF staff and the board rely heavily on the reference of the local pastor or religious leader to select out trustworthy persons for their clients. At the time of visiting, TBF had no complementary savings programme associated with their lending activities. However, as with other board-driven programmes, TBF seeks to minimize its risks as a lender by lending to a cross-section of entrepreneurs, preferably to going concerns when larger loans are being considered. As a result, approximately one half of TBF loans are of US$1,000 or more, and the balanace below this amount.

The style of this Indian CIGP is a mixture of cautious business practice and sincere concern for the welfare of the beneficiaries sought from among the community of the poor. Not only are loan proposals examined in minute detail, but the TBF programme itself is subject to rigorous and regular auditing and progress review against predetermined benchmarks. Project impacts in terms of changes in client incomes, jobs created and of management information are monitored and analysed with the discipline and regularity few other programmes would or could choose to sustain. However, having chosen to operate as a board-driven programme, TBF internalizes the bulk of the transaction costs associated with its credit programme. For TBF there are few alternatives to ensure efficient management and smooth day-to-day loan assessment and monitoring procedures.

An innovation that TBF has entered into involves collaboration with partner NGOs in Bangalore, India, to improve the profitability of the scavenging enterprises that are the livelihood for tens of thousands in that city. Called the rag-pickers project, this is a long-term initiative with an expected duration of 12 years, whose primary beneficiaries are the individuals, mostly male youths aged from 8 years to the mid-20s, many of whom are married with dependent families, who scour the rubbish bins and gutters for textile refuse, paper, rubber, metal, glass, plastics and discarded timber for sale to collection agents.

The project has established a collection agency that competes for supplies at prices that are no higher than those advertised by the 300 established operators in Bangalore. The collection agency then on-sells to the 36 wholesalers in recycled refuse in the city. What the project offers co-operating scavengers that is different is honest weights and measures and access to associated community-development programmes such as informal literacy and skills training, primary health-care and an environment in which the rag-pickers can experience companionship and fellowship. The homeless youth that are the foundation on which this trade is built are not only at the very base of the Poverty Pyramid but their social and emotional deprivation is so intense that the fellowship and protection found in the companionship of peers is an important part of their bondage to traditional operators in the trade.

TBF's role in the rag-picker project is to provide Rs1,425,370 (approx. US$110,000) to the project, which for legal purposes is called refundable aid. This is estimated at 32 per cent of the total project cost, and only Rs588,100 go towards the establishment of the rag-picker enterprise. Rp602,650 go towards social welfare and the balance of the budget to project monitoring and evaluation. TBF's financial contribution forms the basis of the project's working capital, and the source of loans to the enterprises created to operate collection centres and loans made by the collection centre managers to scavengers for working capital purposes. It is through such loans that commercial operators have been able to tighten the bond they have on the collections of individual scavengers, but the rag-pickers are vulnerable because they also need loans to provide the cash flow essential to pay the bribes, entry fees and safety money that are the costs of their employment. It is not unusual for a collection agent to extend more credit for these purposes than is actually necessary in order to tie the borrower to the agent in a bond of debt that can never, in normal circumstances, be loosed. TBF is also involved in promoting a savings programme that will offer the rag-pickers an inflation adjusted real rate of return on their deposits.

The project commenced in July 1984. It has not been easy going as the existing operators have sought to mobilize official and unofficial obstacles to the viability of the enterprise. The project has had to relocate its collection depot several times and suppliers have been intimidated both by police and persons connected with competitors in the industry. However, after several years of operation the project is continuing and is making profits that are ploughed back into the associated community development aspects of the project. Much has been learnt about the trade in that time and this has enabled the operators to improve their approach, essentially by emulating the legitimate practices of those already in the business. By the end of 1987 it was estimated that earnings of the pickers had increased from less than Rs200 a month to more than Rs500 and that some 2,600 persons, including the families of the pickers, are benefiting from this improvement in earnings rate.

KREP: Kenya Rural Enterprise Project, Kenya, Nairobi
This project is indicative of the variety of models that is possible and work in the CIGP arena. Funding for the project comes from USAID but all operational matters are the responsibility of KREP, an NGO established for the

purpose. In turn KREP supports other local NGOs, each of which operates a credit programme to promote microenterprises. KREP is, therefore, an example of the umbrella-model approach, but it is also board driven and harbours goals of community development and financial intermediation between the formal and the informal economy that give it a strong claim to begin a broker-model programme too.

KREP grew out of the USAID funded PISCES experiments and uses the principles identified in the PISCES reports (see Ashe, 1985a). KREP remains an experiment, extending an individual-lending credit programme into the wholesaling of minimal red-tape microenterprise investment finance, complemented by relevant training, technical assistance and financial back-up from KREP. KREP is well on its way toward its programme goal of 20 co-operating NGOs operating CIGPs for the direct benefit of 7,000 micro-entrepreneurs by the end of 1990. At the end of 1987 CIGP programmes were in place with 14 NGOs, there were no loan defaults and the on-time repayment rate was around 80 per cent. Based on past experience with small-enterprise credit programmes in Africa, which have an unenviable but almost universal reputation as financial disasters, this record is magic (see Bigelow et al., 1987).

KREP is not a minimalist CIGP. Training has become a hallmark. Since its inception in mid-1984, 225 staff from 40 local NGOs have participated in workshops covering a wide variety of topics relating to business skills, market surveys, accounting practices, personnel management, credit programmes and microenterprise assessment methods. If demand for places in these courses is a measure of their perceived worth among NGOs in the field, then there is room for more of the same.

By the close of 1987, KREP had extended loans for funding of CIGPs to fourteen local NGOs. Each of these NGOs has the capacity to on-lend at a rate which indicates that 2,173 loans averaging US$1,200 will have been made to individual micro-entrepreneurs and a further 256 loans to group enterprises by the end of 1989. Half of the immediate beneficiaries of these loans are women. If we include dependants and the project-estimated employment creation rate of one job per Ksh1,600 loaned, the total number of beneficiaries is estimated at 45,000 persons, the majority of whom are in the bottom two levels of the Poverty Pyramid.

NCCK: National Christian Council of Kenya

Since 1985 the NCCK, a Nairobi-based NGO, has been one of the beneficiaries of the Kenya Rural Enteprise Project (KREP). It is an integrity-model programme, with some community-development model overtones. It began its CIGP activities in 1981, with something of an inauspicious start. In the period to 1985 on-time repayment rates were at times as low as 50 per cent, and for the five years overall bad debts were rarely less than 10 per cent per annum, rising to a high of 20 per cent in 1984–5. What little information was provided during my visit to the project indicated that NCCK suffered from the limited experience of its staff in the operation of credit-based income-generation programmes, and that its clients suffered financial losses following droughts in 1983–4. Since 1985, NCCK staff have participated in KREP-organized training programmes, and it is anticipated that this will have substantially improved NCCK's capacity for project selection, assessment and monitoring.

Access to unpublished data on NCCK's progress in the period since 1985 proved largely impossible to arrange. Review and evaluation data are available to programme personnel, but my visit to the project happened to coincide with an embargo on the release of data to non-project persons by the project director. It was not my impression that it was my visit that had occasioned the embargo, and it was difficult to leave without the impression that the project is once more in difficulties. If this is the case, it underlines the lack of success that has attended programmes that eschew a policy of openness and attempt to 'do it all for their clients'.

NCCK relies on church networks to identify potential borrowers and, at least on the surface, the character reference from the applicant's pastor, priest or religious leader is critical in the client selection process. In practice NCCK goes beyond the character reference in its loan assessment procedures and attempts to complete a fairly thorough business assessment of applications for loans. Consequently, NCCK operates a highly labour-intensive system sensitive to the skills of its staff. With the exception that the programme does not have a restrictive loan collateral policy, the few clients I was privileged to visit in the field did not regard NCCK as greatly different from a bank. On the top-down bottom-up continuum, the NCCK falls clearly in the top-down end of the scale. On the basis of limited data, some review reports seen at the sponsoring agency and field visits with several loan beneficiaries, the impression was formed that NCCK programme transaction costs are largely internalized. It is possible that with every goodwill, NCCK programme staff have fallen prey to what I judge to be the most common cause of credit programme demise — excessive preoccupation with the success of the programme at the expense of increasing the involvement of the clients they are determined to assist.

DTCL: Daraja Trust Company Ltd

The Daraja Trust Company Ltd largely ceased operations in 1986, the victim of many problems (not least that too many of those charged with responsibility for its policies and operating procedures found this too difficult). Of a total loan portfolio of Ksh1.3m, two-thirds has had to be written off as bad debts. However, the current executive chair of the Daraja Board remains confident that the outstanding debts will, in time, be recovered.

DTCL is the classic board-driven programme and highlights the critical importance of the quality of that board if problems are to be avoided. Nonetheless, it remains that the evaluations of DTCL that have been done also point to resource constraints in the project monitoring and client back-up areas as important contributors to Daraja's problems. It is pertinent to note, however, that DTCL did not work with the poorest of the poor. It worked with relatively well-to-do folk, most of whom were at best members of the near poor or not members of the community of the poor at all. The persons to whom DTCL loaned money were meant to be in a position to be able to offer employment to the poor if only they had the finance. Consequently, the average loan size was large when compared to most programmes that target the poor directly. One might be excused for concluding that the DTCL failure seems to reinforce the overall conclusion of this study — it pays to bank on the poor.

VOICE: Voluntary Organizations in Community Enterprise

VOICE is of interest to this study not because it is responsible for CIGPs in Zimbabwe but because as the umbrella organization of NGOs in that country, in 1985 it conducted a nationwide survey of the income-generation activities and experiences of NGOs. Some its findings, reported in Else

(1987), are valid not only for Zimbabwe but for developing countries in general.

John Else's report for VOICE found 1,688 groups operating income-generation projects in Zimbabwe, supported by 34 NGOs. On average each NGO-supported group is reaching out to 50 or so beneficiaries, or 100,000 people. These numbers seem impressive but in fact they indicate that less than 1 per cent of the country's population are beneficiaries. On a global scale the proportion of people being assisted by income-generation projects is probably well below even this low level.

CIGPs in Zimbabwe continue to be perceived as welfare and reconstrution programmes, a tag that characterized the work of NGOs and co-operatives immediately after the close of sixteen years of armed struggle for independence, achieved in 1980. Consequently, only 18 per cent of the loan programmes surveyed by John Else charged their clients a rate of interest for loans extended, the median size of which is only Z$600 (approx. US$170). The programmes that do charge a rate of interest charge a highly subsidized rate, averaging only 5 per cent, reducing. Consistent with this view, 91 per cent of income-generation projects were found to eschew a minimalist approach to credit for microenterprises and opted for complementary training programmes and technical assistance emphasizing management and leadership skills in addition to loans to clients. The welfare and reconstruction characteristics of these programmes is further confirmed in that only 12 per cent of the 7,768 projects considered in the survey were rated as 'highly profitable', another 65 per cent were considered 'only just profitable', and the balance were 'not profitable'. Overall, the Else report found that the expectations of CIGPs in Zimbabwe are too low, which 'warps the concet of self-reliance'.

In contrast to successful CIGPs visited in other countries, the typical programme in Zimbabwe appears to be top-down, staff-led and NGO dependent. The programme principals attempt to guide their clients into areas of microenterprise investment that they judge a good bet rather than allowing those who have the survival skills essential to life in the poor lane — the intended beneficiaries themselves — to identify their own investment opportunities. As a result CIGPs in Zimbabwe have directed their clients into a limited range of enterprises, such as school-uniform making, with the result that competition has increased with supply and profit margins been shaved till they are non-existent. The VOICE survey found that a mere 15 product areas accounted for 94.3 per cent of the 7,768 income-generation projects examined. The report's concluding observation is telling:

> That the most profitable projects had a higher percentage investment from the members themselves argues for IGP groups starting as savings clubs, which both teach basic business skills and test the seriousness of their interest in establishing businesses. (Else, 1987:6)

ZPT: Zimbabwe Project Trust

The Zimbabwe Project Trust is a welfare organization founded in 1978 which, through its revolving loan fund, provides credit to collective co-operatives with the intention that a financial track record is established for the members. Most of the members are 'former combatants of the liberation armies returned from Mozambique, Zambia and Botswana'. The financial track record is intended to provide them with a ladder into the formal financial system operating in the economy. In this respect ZPT is an umbrella model supporting a number of member co-operatives each of which is seen as operating on the broker model. At the end of 1987 there were some 800 collective co-operatives with a membership of 25,000 persons, between one-third and a quarter of whom are ex-combatants.

Collective co-operatives are meant to be profit-making productive enterprises in which the means of production, essentially land and equipment, are owned and controlled jointly by their members. Title to a co-operative's assets is by equal shares, control is exercised democratically and earnings are distributed on a relatively equal basis on the precept of 'to each according to his work'. The most significant and active of the collective co-operatives are engaged in agriculture (284 registered representing some 90,000 people), mining (25 registered with 1,600 members) or fishing (of which there are many because it is so easy to enter the industry but equally easy to exit, with the result that data on numbers in fishing are regarded as highly unreliable).

A critical source of finance for the collective co-operatives is the estimated 5,500 self-help savings clubs, or RoSCA schemes, that operate at village level across Zimbabwe. It is believed that more than 90 per cent of the members of the savings clubs are women, with each RoSCA having 15–30 members. The ZPT has sought to harness widespread familiarity with the RoSCAs by encouraging their establishment at the co-operative level. Each RoSCA is limited to ten members, each contributing Z$10 a month, with the first recipient receiving a loan of Z$90 to be repaid in monthly instalments of Z$10 in addition to the regular savings commitment.

Over the years the ZPT credit programme has evolved into a risk-end, soft window (zero interest rate and 20 per cent bad-debt ratio), long-term (five years) source of investment finance for the co-operative sector in Zimbabwe. The average loan per co-operative may look large (US$1,800 plus) but on a membership basis this is not so. Moreover, loans from ZPT are not normally given in cash but in kind by the direct purchase on behalf of the client of the required inputs or services for which finance is sought. ZPT is, therefore, not only using the RoSCA model to deliver its services, but also the broker and the merchant models.

From 1983 to 1987, 47 per cent of ZPT's investment and production loans went to agriculture co-operatives, 26 per cent to support co-operative enterprises in the retail field, 13 per cent to industry and 9 per cent to services. In each of these areas ZPT suffered dismal rates of return. The highest bad debts were in the retail area (23 per cent) but loan rescheduling was required for 63 per cent of loans extended to agricultural enterprises.

These performance figures confirm three general observations that can be made about CIGPs:

○ Agricultural crop production enterprises are subject to so many more uncertainties not under the control of the operator than is the case for microenterprises in other sectors of the economy, that they are not well suited to member-based, essentially small, revolving loan-fund investment finance schemes of the CIGP sort. Crop production finance requires a capacity to spread the risk sufficiently widely that in the event of a crop failure for no reason under the control of the farmer, for example a drought or flood, the loss does not financially compromise the entire scheme. None of the CIGP models identified in this study inherently has this capacity, goodwill notwithstanding.

94

○ Retail projects are notorious for generating the circumstances of their own demise. The proliferation of corner stores can so increase competition between *sari-sari* enterprises that the combined total income of all *sari-sari* stores in an area declines, resulting in the exact opposite to the increase in income that CIGP loans are intended to achieve.
○ If one has low expectations of clients being assisted, these expectations tend to be self-fulfilling. ZPT does not expect its clients to be able to service commercial loans, because its beneficiaries are believed to be in a pre-capitalist stage of development, or to have to shoulder the full risks of their investment decisions. The ZPT literature says as much, their reputation precedes them and the expectations of those who come to them for investment loans confirm the necessity of ZPT's most altruistic motives! A reputation of this sort is difficult to escape, but escape it must if ZPT is to remain viable into the long term.

ZWB: Zimbabwe Women's Bureau

This local NGO had its origins in the desperate state of Christian women in rural Zimbabwe at the time of the war for independence. Not only was the social overhead infrastructure minimal, with no government schools, hospitals, for example, but rural women also had no structure through which to provide one another with mutual support, material, emotional and intellectual. ZWB's primary goal, therefore, was to foster women's groups and to act as an umbrella development organization to assist local women's NGOs, including the Girl Guides and Church-based groups. Its CIGP programme was added to its range of activities in 1982.

By the beginning of May 1988, ZWB's credit activities were operating in 13 regions of the country and support had been given to 335 projects, 185 of which were in various agricultural production enterprises in horticulture (130), animal husbandry (31), small-scale irrigation (14) or forestry (10). All loans and projects were group based and the beneficiaries had to complete a preliminary twelve-month programme of training, group meetings, mutual support activities and savings targets (5 per cent of the amount to be borrowed) before becoming eligible for a ZWB loan. Thereafter, ZWB makes it its business to find another financial

95

supporter to take over the on-going task of financial inter-mediation needed by the group. Its success at this has not been great and repeat loans to groups are an increasing feature of ZWB's loan portfolio.

Unlike the Zimbabwe Project, ZWB insists that its loans carry a significant rate of interest (5 per cent in 1987), that member groups contribute a membership fee consistent with value for service and that it has a range of charges it asks members to pay for training and consulting services. These charges are part of ZWB's policy of increasing self-reliance and independence from annual donor grants.

DMWCS: Dondolo–Mudonzvo Women's Credit Scheme
This umbrella organization was created in 1985 to raise funds to support the CIGP activities of other women's NGOs in Zimbabwe, including ZWB. It had made loans to 131 NGOs by May 1988, specializing in loans to NGOs supporting groups that encouraged women to invest in sewing and school-uniform making enterprises. This policy decision betrays its top-down *modus operandi*, and ultimately contributed to an on-time repayment rate that had slipped to 30 per cent, despite the strictly commercial relations between DMWCS and the NGOs to whom it had lent funds. The 54 loans made to sewing groups had been made on the assumption that prices for home-made clothing and school uniforms would not change. They in fact plummetted as the output from diligent sewing groups flooded onto the markeet. It has been a sober lesson to DMWCS, but it also points to the dangers associated with a top-down strategy when management and professional skills available to the implementing NGO are inadequate to the task.

The disillusion this experience left with the women in the 54 sewing groups, established and supported on the advice of DMWCS, who were meant to be its beneficiaries — one of whom had estimated that for a year's sewing she had earned $5! — has had a long-term effect that may never be repaired. It is essential that the board and staff of NGOs operating in the CIGP arena recognize that one of their greatest assets is the business acumen of those who know how to survive in the informal economy of the poor. Their expertise should be sought and harnessed rather than spurned. Participatory programmes that tap this source of talent accord their clients the dignity and respect they deserve as experts in their unique world. The sharing of inherited wisdom and lessons of experience are assets that form the foundations of success for solidarity groups, mutual support RoSCAs, and other grassroots approaches to microenterprise support and community development generally.

Market gardening is an important enterprise for many poor women

Construction provides jobs for many women, but at pitiable wages

3: The contribution of NGOs and CIGPs to poverty alleviation

NOBODY REALLY KNOWS how many NGOs there are in the Third World but a recent estimate by the Club of Rome says there are more than 7,000 in India, 3,000 in the Philippines, 1,600 in Brazil, 1,000 in Thailand, 650 in Nigeria, 370 in Kenya, 380 in Peru, 300 in Ecuador, 270 in Indonesia, 220 in Bolivia and 110 in Cameroun (Schneider, 1988a:78–9). Worldwide, therefore, there may well be in excess of 20,000 indigenous NGOs, the greater proportion of which are involved in development projects of one sort or another. Is this enough? Is there a need for more or bigger NGOs? A little speculation is instructive if not very salutary.

Assume, for example, that each of the estimated 20,000 indigenous NGOs in the Third World manages to service 1,000 clients. Moreover, assume that each beneficiary has five dependents and that each loan made results in the creation of one full-time wage-remunerated job. The person filling that job also has five dependents. On these very optimistic assumptions NGOs reach out to 240 million persons in the developing world. This is less than 5 per cent of the population of the Third World! As a proportion of the number of poor people in each of the five levels of the Poverty Pyramid, NGOs are at best reaching 10 per cent of those presently denied access to investment finance by financial institutions in the formal money economy. This number is also not more than 20 per cent of the number counted as the poorest of the poor in the Third World! Clearly there is a far greater effort needed if the potential for poverty alleviation in microenterprise development is to be fully exploited.

The OECD lists about 4,000 NGOs in developed economies in 1981, of which about 2,200 provide 'significant assistance to developing countries' (Asian Development Bank,

1987, Appendix 1). Total grants from NGOs to developing countries were US$3,978m in 1985, up from US$1,446m in 1975. However, the source of funding for the work of NGOs in developing countries is changing. The development assistance funds transferred by NGOs in 1975 came entirely from the private sector but almost one-third of the amount transferred in 1985 (US$1,028m) was sourced from government grants to NGOs for Third World development purposes.

As a proportion of total Official Development Assistance (ODA), the funds spent by NGOs on Third World development represent less than 4 per cent. However, because so little of official aid is directly allocated to the alleviation of systemic poverty, other than as a consequence of trickle down, the development activities of NGOs as a proportion of ODA going directly to assist the poor are very much more important than these percentages seem to indicate. At a guess, the expenditures of NGOs on development for the poor may represent not less than 50 per cent of total foreign aid directly targetted at poverty alleviation in the informal poverty economy of the Third World. It is not an exaggeration, therefore, to say that NGOs play a pivotal role in development for the poor.

The scope of NGO-based credit programmes

It is important to note that the total volume of NGO-administered credit for income-generation project purposes is not known. There are not, as yet, any accurate statistics on a world scale. The fragmentary data presented in Tables 2.2 and 3.1 may, nonetheless, provide some light on the financial scope and structure of some of these programmes.

In terms of the vastness of the financial needs of the poor for access to credit, the numbers in Tables 2.2 and 3.1 are minuscule. It should also be noted, however, that the data are not only incomplete, they are also selective; the average loan size needed to service demand is small (less than US$100 a loan); and that many of these programmes have been in existence for only a few years or less. CIGPs are a relatively new phenomenon in development. Let us hope that these examples herald a period of sustained growth in the flow of more substantial and appropriate credit for the enterprises of the poor in years to come.

Table 3.1 Some of the NGO providers of very small loans*

Organization	Regional focus	No. of loans made (to 1987 or most recent year)	US$ value of loan portfolio	Average loan size US$
IRDP	India	8,400,000	600 million	71
DRI	India	4,300,000	300 million	70
BKK	Indonesia	2,700,000	55 million	21
Accion Int.	L. America	26,486	17 million	640
SCF	Global	11,518	2.3 million	200
IIDI	Global	2,492	2.6 million	1,050
SEDOM	Malawi	1,610	1.6 million	975
WWF	India	32,303	1.2 million	40
SEDCO	Zimbabwe	115	1.0 million	8,700
FINCA	L. America	8,643	521,000	60
MIDAS	Bangladesh	21	520,000	24,750
CARE Int.	Global	3,200	372,000	115
World Vision	Bangladesh	12,887	270,000	20
SEWA Bank	India	1,297	186,255	143
KCB Jua Kali	Kenya	130	162,500	1,250
OEFI	C. America/ Africa	88	159,835	1,820
MEDA	C. America	359	140,000	400
PfP (WID)	Kenya	2,141	1145,150	65
KCB Jua Kali	Kenya	76	90,350	1,189
DMCS	Zimbabwe	122	49,000	400
SEEDS	Sri Lanka	562	33,000	59
FFHF	C. America/ Africa	438	30,000	70
TARD	Bangladesh	241	11,000	45
REAL	India	125	3,077	38

* Some of these programme specialize in relatively large loans to groups that on-lend much smaller loans to members.
Sources: Dasgupta, 1987; Farnsworth, 1988; McGinnis, 1988; Moloney, 1985; Ruigu, Alila and Mwabu, 1987; Williams, 1986; plus personal communications and various annual reports; specific sources available on request.

While a great number of NGOs are involved in community development, only a small sub-set is active in giving small loans to entrepreneurs in the microenterprise informal poverty economy for income- and employment-generation purposes. Table 2.2 records only a sample of this sub-set. The professional development and NGO literature records others. Those for which basic data on size of loan portfolio and average loan size have been found in that literature are listed in Table 3.1.

This list adds to our stock of data but it too is not exhaustive. Nonetheless, Tables 2.2 and 3.1 do, I believe, cover the major programmes in terms of size but are sure to represent only a fraction of the full population of CIGPs extant in the Third World. The purpose here is not to be comprehensive but to allow the reader to see that despite the proliferation of programmes, this is not enough if a significant impact is to be made on poverty. An explosion of CIGP programmes is both necessary and justified.

The impact of NGO-sponsored CIGPs on the poor

It is often difficult for those who are not in poverty to readily conceive of how the small loans provided by NGO-sponsored income-generation projects can have such a dramatic effect on the fortunes of the poor. There is a degree of scepticism that inevitably attends what can easily be branded as anecdotal exceptions. The reality is quite different.

The financial needs of existing and aspiring entrepreneurs in the informal poverty economy have been neglected for so long that those who are able to bridge the finance constraint reap substantial benefits. My own back-of-the-envelope estimates, based on interviews with clients of programmes visited, confirm the impressive rates of return that have been documented by Wilkinson (1985), BRAC (1987) and others. One or two practical examples may help to illustrate this.

Case 1: Rickshaw driver, Dhaka, Bangladesh
  (a) Before the loan:

Daily earnings	Taka50
less	
Rickshaw rental	Taka20
Rickshaw repairs	Taka5
Daily surplus for living	Taka25

  (b) After the loan:

Daily earnings	Taka50
less	
Rickshaw loan repayment	Taka5
Rickshaw repairs	Taka5
Daily surplus for living	Taka40
Increase in daily income	Taka15
	[i.e., +60 per cent]

        Value of secondhand rickshaw   Taka3,500
        Amount borrowed   Taka3,000

Case 2: Ice maker, Singaraja, Bali, Indonesia
  (a) Before the loan:
        Underemployed, part-time fuel merchant with
        family of five dependants.

  (b) After the loan:
        Borrowed Rp350,000 to buy a refrigerator/freezer
        and insulated containers in order to manufacture
        and sell icey-poles in the hot dry season. Each icey-
        pole sells at Rp25 and distribution is by children
        who sell them at a commission of Rp5 each.
        Estimated net profit was Rp150,000 per month.
        Loan fully repaid in four months.

Case 3: Spare parts recycling co-operative, Solo, Indonesia
  (a) Before the loan:
        140 members in the group
        Average number of employees per member — 2
        @ Rp2,000 a day
        Average net income per member — Rp400,000 a
        month.

  (b) After the loan:
        Group loan of Rp24m distributed to 120 mem-
        bers as working capital loan for an average duration
        of 11 weeks @ interest rate of 3 per cent a month,
        flat.
        Group membership increased to 180 in two years.
        Average number of employees per member in-
        creased to 3 @ Rp3,000 a day.
        Average net income per member increased by 10
        per cent.
        Negligible default rate.

Case 4: Jewellery electroplating, Manila, Philippines
  (a) Before the loan:
        Borrower is a widow with five children. The en-
        terprise is the brainchild of her eldest son, a
        singleton in his late teens at the time the business
        was launched.
        Self employed, working with family members only.

Average family income from business Peso1,000 per month.

(b) After the loan:

A loan of Peso20,000 was taken up in 1987. This was repaid within the year and a second loan of Peso30,000 was received in 1988.

130 persons were apprenticed to the business, 100 of whom had developed sufficient skills to set up as independent operators by February 1988. The remaining 30 worked on a part-time basis doing work on consignment.

Sales of the electroplated jewellery increased 20-fold, with firm contracts negotiated with several of the largest department stores in Manila.

Monthly income of the principal borrower's family has increased to an average Peso15,000 a month. The family has since become bankable.

Case 5: Balut (boiled fertile egg) producer, Valenzuela, Philippines

(a) Before the loan:

Full-time homemaker without cash income in a family of eleven members.

(b) After the loan:

Borrowed Peso20,000 in the first instance and another Peso20,000 in order to expand the business further. By February 1988 she had rented a hen-house fitted with rice-husk driven ovens. At full production she is able to handle 20,000 eggs for a saleable output of 3,000 balut a day.

Sells 80–90 balut to each of 12 regular street vendors for Peso2.95 an egg who retail them at Peso3.75. She supplies two dealers who take 1,100 between them per day. Unfertile eggs are sold at Peso2 each.

Her profit margin per egg is an average six centavos, Peso180 a day, which is about three times the going daily wage rate for women in manufacturing establishments in the area.

With her husband's earnings, the balut business has made a big difference to her and the ten dependants in the family. A portion of the earnings from the enterprise is given to support a local orphanage set up by families in the district to care for children 10 years old and younger who otherwise must seek their survival on the streets of Valenzuela.

Case 6: Retailing expansion loan to add refrigerated goods capacity, Bangalore, India
(a) Before the loan:
Tuck-shop operator on school premises earning Rp700 a month during the school year.

(b) After the loan:
Borrowed Rs10,000 (approx. US$800) for a two-year period to establish a second retail food outlet, fitted with refrigerated capacity to handle the sale of frozen meat, poultry, eggs, butter, milk, etc.

Employed one person at Rs500 a month plus food and drink.

Net family income has increased to Rs4,000 per month.

Loan was repaid ahead of time.

The impact of CIGPs

For the reasons indicated above, at this time it is paticularly difficult to assemble accurate and comprehensive data on the economic and financial impact of NGO credit-based income-generation projects on the poor. Some, but not all of the programmes described in this study have been the subject of professional analysis and impact evaluation. Reports from these studies have been examined when they have been available. Many of these are private and only available in mimeo form; they are important sources for much of the data recorded in Table 3.2. The disparate and unconventional sources of much of this data give it a heterogeneous quality that can obscure the broad picture they support. Consequently, some general observations suggested by the data are worth highlighting:

o Where there are project-level statistics on the impact of small loans on the income of borrowers they are overwhelmingly positive and apear to be very significant.
o The few internal-rate-of-return studies done and reported indicate that CIGPs may be the most profitable way in

105

which society can invest its scarce development funds. Diminishing returns have not yet set-in in this field of development assistance.

○ If on-time debt repayment rates are any sort of indicator of programme effectiveness, then these data also confirm that banking on and with the poor is a very good thing to do for development generally and the alleviation of poverty in particular. Figures on bad debts are notoriously difficult to find but there was nothing to indicate that programmes with on-time repayment rates, defined as payments in accord with the originally negotiated repayment schedule of 80 per cent plus, carried bad debts of any significance. This is not so for programmes where the on-time repayment rate falls below this level.

○ The employment-generation data suggest that Third World governments interested in employment generation should not ignore loans to the poor. Not only do such loans appear effective in this respect, but they generate more jobs more cheaply. In the modern sector it is not unusual for job creation projects to demand an investment of US$10,000 per sustained wage-paying position created. The typical successful CIGP examined in this study and for which job creation data were available indicates an investment well below US$1,000 per sustained wage-paying position created.

○ The impact of CIGPs on the livelihood and prospects of the poor is dramatic rather than marginal. The reasons for this are likely to reflect two factors: the serious under-investment in the microenterprises of the poor in most Third World countries; and when one is living at the margin of survival earning around US$1 a day, an increase in earning capacity of 50 cents a day represents a substantial improvement in cash flow and the capacity to act on the range of economic choices available for investment, saving and consumption.

Table 3.2 summarizes the outcomes from evaluations of the performance of more than two million loans to microenterprises. The 30 or so independent studies on which Table 3.2 is based show an impact on the regular income of borrowers that typically exceeds 20 per cent. Moreover, the studies indicate a level of job-creation potential at a cost per wage-paying position created that marks CIGPs as far more

106

efficient in this respect than equivalent efforts in the modern sector. The limited data also indicate that the cost–benefit ratios, internal rates of return and social accounting studies done in CIGPs reveal benefits to society well in excess of the opportunity cost of investment in additional modernization of Third World economies.

Table 3.2   Indicators of impact on the poor of CIGPs

Project details	Impact indicator	Source
(a) Bangladesh		
Grameen Bank, World Bank Study	(a) Average increase in income from 800 loans 28% pa (b) On-time repayment rate 98% (c) Mobilised $7 million in savings (this is equal to one months wages per borrower)	Blayney and Otero, 1985; Levitsky, 1988
Grameen Bank Independent studies by sponsoring banks	Survey of 825 borrowers in 1980–1 found that income had increased, on average, by 66% as a result of loans made	Mann, Grindle and Shipton, 1989
Grameen Bank	Survey of borrowers 1982–5, found that the average per capita income of loanees increased in real terms from Tk1762 to Tk2697 — 53% in 1982 prices	Yunus, 1988
Bangladesh	Enterprises surveyed in the small and cottage sector, two-thirds appeared to have a modal rate of return to investment of 50% per annum	Tinberg, 1988
Oxfam, Bangladesh	Study of the small credit schemes of 18 NGOs found the following returns on investments by the poor: <table><tr><td>*Item*</td><td>*US$ invested*</td><td>*Return pa (%)*</td></tr><tr><td>Poultry</td><td>0.30</td><td>200</td></tr><tr><td>Money lending</td><td>6.45</td><td>300+</td></tr><tr><td>Sewing machine</td><td>80.65</td><td>250</td></tr><tr><td>Weaving</td><td>266.65</td><td>50+</td></tr><tr><td>Tubewells</td><td>322.60</td><td>400</td></tr></table>	Wilkinson, 1985
CCDB, Bangladesh	(a) Average increase in income of borrowers exceeds 25% (b) On-time repayment rate 97% for small loans and 85% for medium-size loans (c) >60% of loans to women	JVR*

Table 3.2   Continued

Project details	Impact indicator	Source
BRAC, Bangladesh 1987	(a) On-time repayment rate >90% (b) Based on 15,000 loans made in 1986-7, average impact on income by type of firm per 100 Taka borrowed: small trading +250% rice husking +115% transport +91% animal husbandry +36% fishing +30% rice milling +25% (c) Savings of borrowers now totals 50% of the accumulated revolving credit fund (i.e., T30m compared to T60m); 43% of savings are from women borrowers	Van Leeuwen, JVR
(b) India Calcutta, Phase II Urban Development, World Bank Study	Average increase in income from 631 small loans 60% pa	Blayney and Otero, 1985
IRDP, India	An independent evaluation of 1440 beneficiaries in 36 selected districts during January–March 1987 by 27 independent co-operating research institutions found: (a) 64% of beneficiaries increased their annual family income by 50% or more (b) 70% of the assisted families belonged to the poorest of the poor group; however, their share in benefits or IRDP is only 29% (c) In 71% of cases, the assets procured by the IRDP beneficiaries were found intact after two years; this is contrary to the conventional wisdom that beneficiaries of CIGPs dispose of their assets within a short time (d) 43% of beneficiaries had no overdues and a further 32% had overdues of less than Rs1000	Dasgupta, 1987
SEWA Bank, India	Bank of India did a survey of 2000 comparable borrowers of SEWA and several nationalized banks in India and found that SEWA had an on-time repayment rate of 87% compared to only 16% for the commercial banks	Dasgupta, 1987; Sebstad, 1982

Table 3.2 Continued

Project details	Impact indicator	Source
World Vision, India	Average increase in income from 150 small loans >160% pa	Finney, 1988
(c) Sri Lanka		
World Vision, Sri Lanka	(a) On-time repayment rate on loans from Revolving Loan Funds in 700 villages >90% (b) Default rate on rural loans 5% compared to default rates of up to 86% for government loans to the rural sector, 1967–81	Jacobi, 1988; JVR*
(d) Philippines		
PBSP, MMLP	(a) Average increase in income of 41% from average loan amount of US$94– (b) 80% of loans to women (c) Average 5.7 dependants per borrower	de Chavez *et al.*, 1987; JVR
PBSP, 1987–8	(a) Average increase in income reported by 7089 borrowers of 33% from average loan amount of US$112 (b) Estimated 17 924 jobs created at a cost of US$133 job in loans	PBSP Annual Report
TSPI, Philippines	(a) Average increase in income of borrowers +30% (b) On-time repayment rate >80% and bad debts <5% (c) 2718 jobs created @ US$380 lent per job (d) 75% of loans to women (e) Each borrower has average 6 dependants	JVR*
(e) Indonesia		
Bank Rakyat, Indonesia	On-time repayment rate on more than 2 million loans of $5–25 >90%	Bolnick, 1987
YIS, Java	(a) Savings by group members more than double within a year (b) On-time repayment rate >90%	JVR*
MBM, Bali	(a) Average increase in income of borrowers exceeds 30% (b) On-time repayment rate >80% (c) 900+ jobs created @ US$166 lent per job (d) 87% of loans to women	JVR*

Table 3.2 Continued

Project details	Impact indicator	Source
(f) Other		
5 PISCES projects	(a) Benefit: cost ratio >1.0 for each (b) Internal rate of return >100% for 4 out of 5 projects (c) On-time repayment rates >90%	USAID, 1985a
Accion International, PISCES projects	(a) Average increase in income from 26 486 loans >30% pa (b) 1 full-time job for every $1100 lent — less than 1/10th the cost in the modern sector (c) On-time repayment rate >90%	Farnesworth, 1988; Levitsky, 1986
Peru	Average increase in income from 6200 loans, 29% pa	Blayney and Otero, 1985
Dominican Republic Revolving Loan Fund	(a) Average increase in income from 101 loans 27% pa (b) Job creation rate among borrowers >20 times that of control group of non-borrowers	Blayney and Otero, 1985
Costa Rica, Revolving Loan Fund	(a) Average increase in income from 450 small loans >100% pa (b) A new job created for every US$1000 lent	Ashe, 1985

* Based on data gathered during field visits. Specific sources available upon request.

Despite the many thousands of microenterprise loans on which the impact data in Table 3.2 are based, these data remain anecdotal and but a small sample of total activity in the field. Nonetheless, the statistics clearly point in the right direction — CIGPs work for many NGOs and for many poor people. Moreover, the impact of credit to the poorest of the poor on their livelihood and prospects is dramatic rather than marginal.

The dramatic nature of many of the findings reported above may well reflect the lack of attention given to the poor and the serious underinvestment that characterizes the marginalized survival economy in which they live. As the level of underinvestment is reduced we should expect the social and private rates of return to investment in microenterprises to fall towards those that characterize investment in traditional infrastructure and modern-industry investments in the formal economy. Nonetheless, it does not seem too bold to conclude that, as an exercise in wealth creation and self-reliance for and by the poor, CIGPs work very well and are worthy of substantially increased support.

Some observations on models of CIGPs

Is there an optimal model?
At the outset of this study a working hypothesis was that there are optimal models for the delivery of CIGPs. One of the conclusions of the study is that there is indeed a range of models for the delivery of investment finance to microenterprise entrepreneurs, but there is no single best model. There are 'horses for courses'. Nonetheless, there are some general guidelines that do seem worthy of particular note.

On the whole the savings-linked models seem to be superior in several important ways to minimalist pure credit-delivery types. In particular, savings link aid in discriminating between potential clients, provide a basis on which programme viability and independence from reliance on foreign-donor support can be built and open the door to offering the poor a real rate of return on their financial deposits.

There are at least six savings-linked models on which one could call in implementing a CIGP programme. Which one is optimal will depend entirely on what is the full complement of goals set for the programme. It would appear that programmes that are directed at persons at the lowest three levels of the Poverty Pyramid are significantly advantaged if they are not only savings-linked but also group-based and are able to exploit the discipline of peer group and community pressure.

In the upper rungs of the Poverty Pyramid the role of a CIGP is more likely to be concentrated on the provision of expansion loans to existing enterprises. A minimalist approach to credit delivery may not be the most desirable at this level of economic activity. Skilled staff, complementary capacity within the programme, possibly from among board members, to undertake project and market analysis and an ability to arrange appropriate training can pay handsome dividends once one reaches out beyond the simple esoterics of the one-person firms that dominate the survival activities at the extremes of poverty.

One unequivocal message of this study regarding models is that no CIGP programme will succeed if it does not use the model most appropriate to its client groups. There are very few programmes that operate on the basis of a single model. Most programmes tailor their delivery mechanisms to suit the levels of enterprise being targetted, with a different approach taken towards the making of the smallest compared to the largest loans. This is in keeping with the heterogeneity of the community of the poor and consistent with sound business practice. A diversity of financial intermediation mechanisms is just as appropriate to the world of poverty as it is to the economy of the rich.

The importance of training
In many respects it is not the CIGP model that is critical; it is what works well that counts. Different approaches are needed for programmes directed at different levels of enterprise in the informal poverty economy. At the survival level, the lowest end of the Poverty Pyramid, there appears to be little to be gained from incorporating borrower-directed training programmes, enterprise- or sector-based feasibility studies or legal contracts into project procedures. At this level of enterprise, poverty is so pressing that businesses cannot afford to be too inefficient and the discipline of peer-group pressure plus the carrot of repeat loans to borrowers with a good repayment record seems to be sufficient inducement to ensure that borrowes do all they are able to protect their access to additional loans. Logic and casual observation suggest that at the lowest levels of the Poverty Pyramid there are more productive outlets for the scarce financial and personnel resources available to CIGP programmes than the provision of formal training in basic business skills. This conclusion is reinforced by the fact that many survival-level enterprises, especially in Latin America, operate outside the letter of the law. Typically survival enterprises that employ the vulnerable and labouring poor are not registered, do not conform to local workplace regulations, eschew any reporting to government agencies and operate at such a wretched level that there is little from which official taxes and charges could be paid after the expenses of doing business have been met. In these circumstances the entrepreneur cannot afford to make too many mistakes, nor is it beyond her or his capacity to carry the essential knowledge of the business' assets, liabilities, stocks and customers in the head. For the many thousands of women who find in microenterprises a fulfilling

and productive avenue to personal cash income, this secrecy can be essential if they are to retain control of the income that the enterprise is able to generate. They have no need of written records and financial accounts.

Above the survival level things become more complicated. Record keeping, cash management and personnel skills become more important the bigger the microenterprise becomes. At these higher levels of business, productivity responds more readily to formal management skills than it does when the firm is small enough for details of sales, stocks, suppliers, debts and creditors to be a matter for one's memory. At these higher levels the returns to investment of formal training in business skills may justify the allocation of funds in that direction.

It does not follow however, that as the size of enterprise being assisted increases beyond the survival level a formal set of subsidized training programmes is the only way to go for programme success. Some programmes have developed around group systems of CIGP implementation and monitoring. These lend themselves very readily to informal 'on the job' style training. Some of the more common informal learning-while-doing mechanisms are peer review within the context of group activities, problem discussion sessions during scheduled formal group meetings, mutual support during times of personal or family crisis or business failures, and the sharing of the benefits that flow from access to the group's wider information base. Many of these informal training activities will occur naturally, but others require the guiding hand of a project worker if they are to be effective. This is especially so where cross-group fertilization is to be tapped for motivational training, vision expansion or experience sharing.

Some solidarity-group programmes, such as the Grameen Bank and BRAC in Bangladesh, go so far as to direct that the group devote a proportion of its savings to training in areas that group members judge important enough to justify the cost. The areas of training chosen by the groups have not always referred to business skills. In the first instance they are most likely to identify literacy, primary education for the children or health and infant welfare as priority areas before a decision is taken to invest in human capital that is purely business focused. Other CIGPs, such as KREP in Kenya, insist that where possible subsidies for business and management-skills training are minimal and groups be required to make a contribution towards training offered in order to weed out training activities that are meeting a real need from those that programme principals think their client partners need.

Formal training programmes seem to be critical in the case of the board-driven approach to CIGP implementation. In the main the board-driven models seek to help the poor by generating additional job opportunities through the expansion of going concerns. Consequently, the complementary training needs of a board-driven CIGP are of three types:

○ Training to ensure that programme personnel are technically competent in accounting, investment analysis, project appraisal and various other management and people skills. The more that the programme internalizes the transactions costs of implementing a CIGP, the more critical it is that loan-programme staff be technically first rate.

○ Non-traditional training directed at board members themselves. Board members need to be motivated and imbued with the shared philosophy behind the programme. This may involve board retreats devoted to a close study of poverty in the regions in which the CIGP is being spread, or an evaluation of medium- and long-term programme goals. The board is also likely to need expert consultation and advice on options open to it in the design of a local programme viability strategy that will wean the indigenous NGO from ongoing dependence on its foreign partner. The latter goes well beyond local fundraising strategies, and challenges the board to rationalize its policies on interest rates, fees for services rendered and long-term versus short-term goals.

○ Training directed at making the clients of business-expansion loans better business persons and better managers. It cannot be assumed that a successful microenterprise entrepreneur will be similarly successful running a much larger small firm. Business problems associated with stock management, personnel management, market analysis, accounting procedures, cash–flow management, banking practices and legal and reporting requirements increase exponentially as the size of the enterprise reaches beyond the survival level. At these higher levels of enterprise in the Poverty Pyramid, it is in the interests of the success of

114

loans made that the CIGP should offer complementary training in these and related areas to its clients.

The advantages of partnership
The board-driven model of a CIGP has some important strengths that should be noted for the attention of programmes that operate largely without the direction of a local board. A strong and principled board of directors brings to the programme a mechanism for handling financial accountability to local and foreign sponsors, greater in-house depth in project monitoring and evaluation, added reporting and documentation skills, greater potential in the mobilization of local resources to underpin a policy of increasing institutional independence and financial viability and an ability for policy formulation and identification of programme expansion strategies that benefit from the business and management experience of individual board members.

In the eyes of foreign donors these are strengths that are especially important if the partner relationship is to thrive. There is also particular merit in local beneficiaries having to account not to the foreign partner, but to the local NGO whose board is respected for its talent, integrity and genuine concern for the poor. In turn it is the board of the local NGO that accounts to its partner agencies, ensuring that the worst features of cultural imperialism are kept at arms length. The problem of programme replication is also one that a local board can oversee far more effectively than a foreign-based NGO or donor agency. The provincial partners of TSPI, the rural development and urban livelihood programme of PBSP, the credit-union creation strategy of Caritas, CULB and TCCS, and the growth of Grameen in Bangladesh are some examples of programmes that have benefited greatly from their partnerships with foreign NGOs. Without these partnerships it must be doubted that the success that some programmes have achieved in replication or programme expansion would have been possible, the wisdom and drive of their respective local boards of directors notwithstanding.

Of brokers and merchants
Two of the more popular models of CIGP delivery are the broker and the merchant models. Almost all programmes examined for this study presented themselves as having embraced the role of broker between the formal financial

institutions in the modern economy and the poor who desire but are denied access to the financial services of these institutions. A substantial number also adopted the protective paternalism that is a primary characteristic of programmes geared up on merchant-model lines. Both models are important for very different reasons, and we would be remiss if we did not pay them some special attention.

There are two forms of the broker model. One is where the NGO seeks to become a substitute financial-lending institution, much as the Grameen Bank has done in Bangladesh. This model is particularly difficult to institute, requires a wealth of talented and committed village-level organizers, but is probably the great challenge in the CIGP domain in the decades ahead. There will be a need for agencies such as the World Bank, the regional development banks and other multilateral agencies to identify ways in which they can use their financial strength to nurture many more Grameen-type NGOs.

The second form of the broker model divides responsibilities for the CIGP between the implementing NGO and the formal banking system in such a way that: the collaborating bank administers programme savings and the money provided for the credit programme (usually a revolving credit fund held as a bank deposit); and the NGO absorbs the transactions costs associated with the processing of loan applications, selection and repayment procedures, and some follow-up microenterprise support activities. The aim is to free the bank from the constraints of high transactions costs but at the same time arrange for bank access to information on potential borrowers that it could not otherwise afford to collect. In this way the CIGP is intended to establish for borrowers a track record in the formal financial sector and so help the CIGP work itself out of a job.

The broker model also has other perceived benefits, including the introduction of poor entrepreneurs to the discipline of formal banking, access by the programme to an established administrative network for the collection of repayments and the implementation of a CIGP-linked savings programme. But these benefits are not costless; they restrict the NGO to areas where banks have branches or representatives, which may not be where the neediest potential borrowers are to be found. The broker model does little to increase the velocity of circulation of cash in the informal poverty economy. The exact opposite is the case if the co-operating banks do not assist by extending loans to small depositors on the basis of their savings. In so far as the savings of the poor are channelled out of the informal poverty economy and into the formal modern economy there is an important loss of liquidity and investment potential available to informal-sector entrepreneurs.

It is a matter of some concern that in all the field-work undertaken for this study, not one broker-model CIGP programme was encountered where the track record established at the bank resulted in a flow of bank-loans from the bank to CIGP programme depositors. Precisely the opposite is the case. In the main, programmes lament the lack of success they are having as brokers! Is this because of a lack of negotiating skills on behalf of programme personnel, reticence on the part of the banks to expand into a non-traditional area of lending or some other reason? The answer as to where the primary constraints lie is not obvious. It is an area worthy of further research.

The most serious problem of all associated with the broker model is that it seems to enable the banks to avoid coming to grips with how they might rearrange their business so as to service the needs of savers and investors in the informal poverty economy more effectively. To the extent that this is so, the broker model is limited in its capacity to be additive in the generation of resource flows to which microenterprise entrepreneurs have access. This is a matter of particular import, as in the long term the poor will remain poor if they continue to be denied access to financial intermediation services. Society is the poorer because socially profitable investments are not being funded in favour of investments that offer society a lower rate of return. Ways ought to be found to rectify this situation and improve the performance of NGOs in their brokering role.

The merchant model is quite a different beast from the broker. The essence of the merchant model is the provision of goods instead of money in response to an application for a loan. Applications are processed, and approved applications are fulfilled by the supply of loans in kind. The theory is that this enforces the borrower to be specific about what the borrowed money is to be used for while also ensuring that the funds are used for the purpose intended.

In many ways the merchant model is a variation of the company shop that pays workers in wage-goods rather than money. The NGOs that employ the system (it is common in Indonesia, the Philippines, India, Africa), claim that it allows them to pass on to borrowers the benefits of lower prices for inputs, greater quality control, the protection of warranty provisions and access to technical advice and follow-up service available to the NGO but difficult for a poverty-stricken microenterprise entrepreneur to organize. These claims may be true, but there are also serious drawbacks to the merchant model that have seen it sow the seeds of its own demise.

The model can institutionalize a lack of trust in the honesty and ability of the poor to manage their own economic affairs. It encourages the notion that the poor are helpless, need protection and cannot be trusted to do what is in their own best interests. The model is also open to abuse by less than scrupulous administrators who see a profit in a captive market. Commissions from favoured suppliers are a classic temptation that has often undermined the integrity of programmes begun with the best of intentions. But most worrying is the rigidity that this sort of system introduces into the decisionmaking of small business persons.

Why should a woman who applies for a tiny loan to upgrade her sewing machine be forced to use the money in this way if, in the meantime, she gains access to a cheap source of material and would prefer to invest in stock to take advantage of a windfall gain? Why shouldn't a borrower be able to divert a part of a loan to a purpose that is productive, for example, the purchase of medicine for family members who fall sick and are important helpers in the enterprise, but not necessarily specified in the original loan application? The essence of business activities by the poor is flexibility and ability to exploit profitable opportunities as and when they arise. The restriction of in-kind loans limits this flexibility in ways that can have undesirable short- and longer-term consequences. Only where there is reason to believe that loan repayment rates will suffer or where some form of countervailing power is essential to ensure that favourable prices are to be passed on to borrowers does there seem to be justification for the use of this tied-aid merchant model. In all other cases it is critical that the programme guard against secret commissions or other inducements to programme principals that, when discovered, encourage borrowers to do likewise and divert a little more benefit their own way by joining the list of debt defaulters.

Women spend many hours collecting wood from far away – for two days work they earn 30–50 cents

4: Summary and conclusions

POVERTY MAY BE an obstacle to economic growth in the Third World, but the poor are not a liability. They are an asset in the fight against poverty so far neglected by the development planners. The poor constitute a market of substantial size in most developing countries that has not been exploited as an engine of growth based on the market for wage-goods. The demand for labour in the poverty sector of Third World economies is no less a derived demand, based on the demand for the goods and services produced in the economy, than is the demand for skilled labour in the modern economy. CIGPs are important because they exploit this simple relationship between the demand for commodities and the demand for labour as the key that unlocks the door that leads to escape from poverty. How CIGPs can be nurtured and promulgated is, therefore, a significant step in the right direction in Third World development.

The secrets of success in credit-based income-generation programmes

The poor are an asset
There is no magic formula or recipe for success. There are, however, rewards for hard work, dedication, common sense, honesty, integrity and openness to the lessons of on-the-job practice. These rewards can be improved if the wisdom of experience is sifted and distilled. Much of that wisdom is in the hands of the entrepreneurs among the poor themselves, the client group that the CIGP programme is intended to assist. The very first and most fundamental point is, therefore, not to spurn the poor but to recognize in them an asset that is the foundation of sustainable success.

Horses for courses

It is possible to identify general guidelines that seem to make income- and employment-generating credit programmes work better. However, there will always remain unique requirements that tailor each programme to its intended target group and socio-economic environment. In what follows there is no pretence that it is possible to devise shortcuts to that process of tailoring. It is a process that depends more on familiarity with the people, the culture, the institutions and the environmental constraints that operate, than on the possession of specific skills in economics, accounting, engineering or any other discipline.

Clear statement of programme goals

Success is a relative concept, one that has little or no meaning outside the context of the objectives sought. Many CIGP programmes embrace goals that are community-wide as well as goals that are person-centred. For these programmes success cannot be gauged simply by considering whether the borrower's income has increased as a result of the loan. Other criteria ought also to enter the definition of success. For our purposes, however, we have had to compromise and use as a working proxy for success:

o a programme's capacity to deliver loans to microenterprise entrepreneurs otherwise unable to borrow from the modern sector
o that loans extended have had a positive impact on income and employment
o that the programme has been able to maintain a high on-time repayment rate
o that loan interest and service charges associated with programme lending are pitched at levels that are competitive with rates charged in the market place; and
o that the programme has a capacity to reach an expanding client population.

Documentation and performance monitoring

A common problem with NGO income- and employment-generation programmes is the poor quality documentation that exists detailing their performance. Although NGOs collect massive amounts of information, very little of it is ever analysed for effective use in decisionmaking or as a base from

121

which others may learn. Many NGOs would be well advised to collect less information, concentrate on monitoring data that are central to the key objectives of their programme and assiduously document those aspcts of the programme that are perceived to be critical performance indicators that management ought to monitor. Some of these indicators might cover the effect of credit provided on client income, employment or savings; cost of delivery of the programme; constraints overcome in expanding the programme to an increasing number of participants; repayment rate by type and size of loan; and lending policy conflicts encountered in implementing the programme.

People-skills critical
It should not come as a surprise to learn that people-skills, the ability to relate to people in poverty, and leadership are the most important personnel skills for successful organization at the grassroots. The effectiveness with which these skills can be used is dependent upon the respect and integrity with which project personnel are received by the client group. If programme participants perceive project personnel as more concerned with what personal gain they can get out of the programme, a similar attitude will be mimicked by borrowers. Corruption breeds corruption, but honesty and integrity encourage the like in return.

A critical people-skill required of programme administrators is the need to distinguish between loan applicants who are genuine entrepreneurs and others. The CIGP is not a therapy group, nor is it a substitute for a clinical rehabilitation programme. It behoves loan staff of the CIGP, therefore, to guard against the unscrupulous and misguided person whose primary interest is to obtain access to the fund to feed an alcohol or some other injurious addiction. The avenues by which this sort of discernment can be gained are limited, but to be forewarned is to be on guard. This is also another reason why it is often highly advantageous to ensure that clients of good standing have a real input into the CIGP's client-selection processes. Solidarity-group systems of CIGP organization are particularly well suited to using the unique intelligence and peer group self-interest as protection against loan defaults from this sort of source; another effective technique is to ensure that the policy-making organs of the CIGP have access to the real-world hard-headed advice of representatives from among its major groups of clients. The Grameen Bank has done this by reserving the bulk of the positions on its board of directors for elected representatives of borrowers (7 of the Grameen Bank's 9 elected directors in 1987–8 were illiterate women, representatives of the 85 per cent of the Grameen borrowers who are women).

What to do to ensure that the impact is sustained
There are both short-term and long-term measures of success. The truly effective projects are those that measure up in both respects. Too often, however, the long-term sustained impact is negligible despite a post-project audit that is laudatory in every respect. There has been very little research done on why this kind of anomaly can arise, but what there is seems reasonably unequivocal in its conclusionss: no matter the context or the type of approach (model) adopted, the most dynamic and successful programmes in the short term (as measured by growth in the number of loans made and level of on-time repayment rate achieved), and those with a sustained positive impact in the long term, are those that relate best to the needs of the people they seek to serve. This is not a unique observation. It has been made before, but bears repeating. Michael Farbman (1981) commenting on the USAID-funded global experiment in small loans for businesses in the informal poverty economy, known as PISCES: Programme for Investment in the Small Capital Enterprise Sector, has written:

> in the most effective projects we found one precept to be universally valid: Programme inputs are responsive to the plans and desires of those they serve and to the degree possible reflect the level of skills and knowledge that commonly exists in the community.

Six years later Michael Cernea (1987) wrote something similar in his review of the sustainability of achievements in World Bank projects. His observations are couched in operational terms, linking the short-term impact of new resource inputs with the need to achieve a sustainable impact on the situation of the poor many years later. After an intensive study of 25 very large World Bank projects he concluded:

> A major contribution to sustainability came from the development of grassroots organizations, whereby project beneficiaries

gradually assume increasing responsibility for project activities
. . . a measure of beneficiary control over the management of
the organization, and the continuing alignment of the project
activities with the needs of the beneficiaries. (p.7)

In other words long-term impact is directly related not
only to the extent to which a project is able to address demand, but also the extent to which the project is pitched at a
level that the beneficiaries find appropriate to their resource
constraints and technological competence. If the assets
brought in by a project are beyond those that the community
can maintain and sustain, or the administrative structures
required for programme implementation are complicated
and beyond the capacity of local people to accept, the project
is unlikely to have an impact in the long term that is consistent with short-term expectations. The latter are based on
performance audit criteria that reflect the impact of resources available during project implementation, which are
typically well in excess of those available from community
resources in the long term. Given the grassroots orientation
of most successful CIGPs, and a commitment to a philosophy that is consistent with the sustainability principles outlined by both Farbman (1981) and Cernea (1987), it is not
unreasonable to expect that because CIGPs share control
over management with programme beneficiaries and target
project activities, especially their lending activities, to the
needs of participants, they will also have a sustained impact
into the long term.

Simple is optimal
Transactions costs are greater the more complex the procedures adopted to implement a CIGP programme. A particularly pernicious obstacle to greater use of existing
financial institutions by the poor is the requirement that substantial collateral and personal references should be offered
as a guarantee for the security of the proposed debt. In order
to implement these requirements the formal financial institutions have developed a complex set of procedures that are
costly and discriminate against the poor. Many NGOs have
sought to overcome these obstacles by chosing loan-
application procedures that focus on simple to administer
proxies for more complex client-selection criteria. Church-
linked credit programmes choose to rely on the reputation

that a potential borrower has for honesty and trustworthiness as the critical proxy variable. Assessment of these qualities is left by the programme to the person's pastor, priest, minister or mullah to determine. If these qualities are said to describe the applicant, then this is all the collateral necessary for a small loan to be granted. The system is simple and appears to work well. Once larger loans are at issue, however, something more tangible than the borrower's reputation is normaly sought.

Other procedures ought also to be simple and conscious of the high opportunity cost of time to poor people operating at the edge of survival. Where possible repayment procedures should not conflict with the regular demands of life; they should reinforce the business goals of the programme, for example, use established financial structures that clients can expect to graduate towards in arranging accounting procedures; and be tied in to peer-reviewed self-monitoring systems of performance assessment. If these conditions can be achieved, and solidarity groups by their very nature are well suited to ensuring that they are, the programme's administrative procedures will act as a positive reinforcement of good business practices rather than an annoying diversion from the borrower's attention to the business at hand.

A business-like approach

There is still some debate as to whether CIGPs should favour the poor with subsidized interest rates and services. There are valid arguments on both sides, but it seems that interest-rate subsidies are not essential to the success of a CIGP. If subsidies are given, the justification should not be to guarantee the success of the programme. In fact the opposite can easily be the case, such as where the existence of an interest-rate subsidy compromises the business-like reputation of the programme by confusing it with welfare dole-outs and softly, softly approaches to the problems of poverty.

The poor live in the school of hard knocks and value nothing more than being treated with dignity and justice. They are used to being taken advantage of because of their lack of bargaining power and position. It is a pleasure to them when they receive value for money and are not denied access to resources on terms similar to those available to investors fortunate enough not to be poor. The poor will also willingly pay for services and technical assistance that they perceive relevant and fairly priced. They are more than happy to pay interest rates that are at market levels. Investors in poverty-sector microenterprises are not so much concerned with the price they have to pay for investment finance as with the lack of access they have to loanable funds for such purposes.

Appropriate programme policies

As with any business, a credit programme must operate on the basis of clearly stated policies. First and foremost there is the interest-rate policy, about which comment has already been passed. There are other policies that will influence programme performance. The most important of these relates to the ability of the programme to respond flexibly and appropriately to the client group and the socio-economic circumstances with which it seeks to deal. For example, policies on loan duration ought not to be set mechanically. Loan conditions, and especially the loan duration, ought to depend upon the nature of the enterprise and the business cycle peculiar to the market in which the enterprise operates. Too often a shortage of trained programme staff results in the adoption of a very narrow range of loan repayment periods, none of which is necessarily related to the essential business cycle of the enterprise being financed. In such circumstances there is a temptation to set arbitrarily the loan repayment period at six or twelve months. In the case of retailing enterprises in which stock turnover is rapid, a much shorter loan period is likely to be more appropriate. On the other hand an animal husbandry enterprise, such as chickens, may find a loan period of nine months more appropriate so long as a repayment grace period applies for the first three or so months until the business begins to generate a cash flow. Management of the credit programme has to be sufficiently flexible, talented and sensitive to ensure that the policy allows for the tailoring of loan conditions to client needs. In the case of a solidarity-group based programme these details can usually be left to the group to determine.

Programme viability and sustainability

Some CIGPs look to the day when they will no longer be needed because they have graduated their target beneficiaries from the informal poverty economy to be serviced by the financial institutions available in the formal modern economy. Other programmes are based on the assumption that they are here for the long haul. Either way, both types of programme must establish definite targets for financial viability and sustainability suited to their long-term intentions. If these intentions include a desire to become independent of a foreign donor, most of whom have a policy of providing aid for a maximum period of five years, a strategy must be identified by which this is to be achieved. Savings-linked programmes have it very much easier in this respect than those that eschew a savings component; similarly, programmes that charge for the technical and consulting services offered to microenterprises have a much easier task ahead of them than those that offer these services free of charge. It will always be difficult, if not impossible, for a CIGP to become financially viable and sustainable if it does not charge interest at market rates.

The programme must not ignore the government policy environment in which it is operating
There is a clear association between programme performance and the policy environment in which it has to operate. A growing economy is more favourable to success than a stagnant or declining one. If the lending programme is to avoid unnecessary risks, it cannot afford not to be aware of the impact that extant or foreshadowed government policies are likely to have on prospects in the microenterprise sector. National food-policy developments and changes in foreign trade restrictions are two areas especially important to the economics of the survival enterprises of the poor. At times it will be in the interests of the programme and its clients that programme resources should be allocated to the lifting or reform of policies that constrain the range of business opportunities open to the poor. This may involve lobbying government for a change in tariff policy or local market regulatory procedures, intervention with the police or local government authorities to put a stop to the constant harassment of the poor, legal action to regularize the tenure of the poor in slum districts, bureaucratic pressure to secure improved access for member communities to potable water, power and sanitation or the provision of specific technical assistance to clarify alternatives open to the government that are less hostile to the poor. Hernando de Soto (1986) in Latin America, SEWA in India (see Sebstad, 1982) and BRAC in Bangladesh have

been in the vanguard of those who believe that legalization of the economic activities of the poor will go a long way towards lifting an important obstacle to self-help avenues of escape from poverty in the Third World. The impact of government policies on the prospects of microenterprises and other vehicles of self-help available to the poor is a much neglected area of Third World economic development, richly deserving of further research.

Some conclusions and policy implications

There is sufficient evidence to indicate that investment in the enterprise of the poor is well below socially desirable levels. Underinvestment has arisen because development and government policies generally have ignored the informal poverty economy in favour of the formal modern sector. Official development policies have biased the cost of capital to the modern sector below its true social opportunity cost. This has encouraged the substitution of capital for labour and forcibly channelled the savings of the poor into modern sector applications. Moreover, there is a serious market failure operating in so far as investment decisions in Third World economies are based on the disinformation that exists about investment opportunities and risks of lending to the poor. Lending to the poor is good business.

On the other hand chronic poverty is not a problem at which one can simply throw money and have it go away. Sustained redress of past biases and revised development strategies designed to make a genuine assault on poverty by helping the poor to help themselves is no simple task. It is not enough to say that we must attack the causes of poverty; we must also remove the obstacles to escape from poverty that keep people poor. Denial of access to investment finance and the general lack of financial intermediation services available to the poor are two of the more important of these obstacles. Resources devoted to CIGPs respond to both of these constraints in an effective and appropriate way.

It is time to recognize that the resource delivery systems of the free market cannot be replicated by the command economy strategies that have been the hallmark of Third World development planning since the 1960s. A new approach is required, one that respects but exploits the atomistic nature of competition in the survival economy of the poor. Poverty

128

alleviation policies must tap the vitality and potential of the private enterprise driven economic goals of the many thousands of small businesses that employ and service the consumption needs of the poor. It is critical that we do all in our power to ensure that public resources are used not to displace the poor but to increase their productivity and the value-added associated with their economic activity.

The impact data on CIGPs presented in the foregoing are at least a cause for great hope. They provide a basis for believing that the impact of successful CIGPs is not only positive to an impressive degree in the short term, but that the benefits will be sustained into the long term also. Despite the anecdotal nature of much of the data, it is clear that the social rates of return to investment in CIGPs warrant the diversion of funds on a massive scale into income- and employment-generation activities by the poor. Some of the more creative CIGPs described above show how that can be done. If this book has done nothing else, I hope that it has demonstrated to the hard headed that the poor are a much neglected investment opportunity.

The level of attention devoted to poverty and the economic problems of the poor is far too little and the volume of resources, financial and human, flowing into programmes that address them too small, drastically below that which their demonstrated impact on the lives of the poor and the estimated rates of return warrant. Moreover, the data indicate that poverty alleviation in the Third World is an attainable goal in our lifetime. What is needed is the courage to allow the poor to help themselves by removing those constraints that institutionalize systemic poverty. Charity to the non-destitute is one of these constraints; denial of access to investment funding another; big government and excessive regulation of every conceivable aspect of the daily lives of Third World peoples yet others. It is hoped, therefore, that this study will add weight to the challenge to the global community to improve the plight and prospects of the poor, that all NGOs, business and professional people, Third World governments, donor-nation governments, aid agencies and financial institutions make the promotion and support of credit-based income-generation programmes a matter of the highest priority for their development policies and assistance.

What sorts of practical steps or actions could be taken towards increasing the priority given to poverty alleviation and CIGPs in particular? Let us consider this question in terms of the major actors on whom the responsibility falls:

Governments
In view of the importance of the problem of poverty alleviation and the proven comparative advantage of NGOs in
working with the poor, it is in the interests of Third World
governments to give every encouragement and support to the
strengthening of NGOs as sponsors and partners in CIGP
initiatives. Official recognition of their role in CIGPs and in
broad-based economic development would assist NGOs in
their struggle to work more closely with commercial banks
and national central banking authorities.

In practice, if not by definition, Third World governments
have not established a tradition or a track record of working
with indigenous NGOs that sponsor or support grassroots
CIGPs. Some assistance to credit unions in some countries is
a possible exception to this observation. Nonetheless, it remains true that government representatives and agencies will
have to tread carefully when seeking to enter this field. The
choice of which NGOs to suport, how to support them and
the way in which public servants can assist in the creation of
purpose-designed CIGP private-sector programmes among
the poor are not trivial problems. Some pointers to answers
to these issues are contained in this book but there is a great
deal more research required before a comprehensive set of
answers can be given. Here it is not possible for me to do
more than highlight some key considerations:

○ a business-like approach is critical in order to establish
  clearly from the outset that the proposed CIGP is not an
  exercise in charity or government handouts
○ an agreed set of goals and achievement indicators must be
  accepted by all parties
○ where possible the administrative and institutional structures adopted should capitalize on the discipline of self-
  interest and peer review; it is almost always coun-
  terproductive for staff of the CIGP to attempt to second
  guess what is best for the potential client
○ all CIGPs should have a business plan that includes consideration of the time-frame and the means by which the
  programme will achieve independent viability

Development-assistance donor governments and their aid agencies could also see it as in their own interests to channel far more of their bilateral and multilateral aid commitments into the support of CIGPs. Financial viability studies prepared by some of the more established NGOs show the need for the injection of external financial aid to match local counterpart funds, if a sound financial base is to be established within five years. With this sort of aid, indigenous NGOs can achieve full financial viability for their CIGPs based on continuing high levels of on-time repayments into the revolving loan fund at market rates of interest and active participation of beneficiaries in interest-bearing savings deposits leading, ultimately, to their participation in the ownership of the programme.

Public investment in improved infrastructure servicing the informal economy is also important, especially where this influences the health and nutrition of the poor. So too is the deregulation of markets so as to allow market forces to operate and encourage entrepreneurship at all levels of the Poverty Pyramid and the economy generally. Particular attention must be directed at areas of the economy where monopoly power is vested in the hands of the few; where these are are public officials administering a government programme or semi-independent parastatal enterprise there exists a special responsibility to examine whether the continued existence of that monopoly advances or hinders the cause of poverty alleviation in the nation.

Non-governmental organizations
The advantages of non-governmental organizations in reaching out to and working amongst the poor are overwhelming. This study contains only a glimpse of their successful track record in establishing, nurturing and eventually divesting ownership of CIGPs on to the poor of the Third World. Their record is a clear pointer to the future. The overwhelming importance of private enterprise in the informal poverty economy gives NGOs a special place and a special opportunity to take the lead in income- and employment-generation initiatives among the poor. It is critical that there be more of the same. Three areas deserve special attention by the NGOs themselves:

○ In view of the limited resource base of NGOs relative to the magnitude of the needs of the poor, NGOs will need to

131

devote more attention to their role as catalysts able to improve the links between the informal poverty economy and the rest of the economy, especially as this bears on access to loanable funds. They need to view themselves as potential bridges or intermediary linkages between self-help groups and the banking community. Special informal poverty-sector subsidiaries of national and international financial institutions may arise, institutions that are willing and able to collaborate with local and foreign NGOs to fill the financial intermediation gap that currently confronts the poor.

○ To become as important as bridges between the poor and the formal economy as they are capable of becoming, many NGOs will have to go beyond rhetoric and act on the veracity of the convictions that they espouse. They must become risk-takers and institutional innovators by seeking to experiment with the creation of new lines of credit for the poor, and borrow on behalf of the clients that they serve from the banks to which the poor now have no access. However, before many NGOs are able to do this, they will themselves have to lift their game; they will need to improve their own professional efficiency and financial accountability and be able to demonstrate, amongst other things, their financial viability, loan-recovery performance, impact on incomes and job creation if they are to have the track record that will be sought after for this important role. I hope that this study will contribute to this process by identifying strengths from successful programmes that can be incorporated into their own.

○ There is a need for many more NGOs to emulate the performance of the Grameen Bank and seek to become more like banks themselves or to foster the establishment and growth of institutions able to do so.

○ The ethics of development must not be abandoned or neglected in capitulation to the anxiety that can be associated with the pursuit of 'job creation' or other goals of the CIGP. Sweatshop conditions or other manifestations of the foundations of systemic poverty are an abuse of the dignity of the very people that the CIGP is intended to assist.

The role of the private sector

The overwhelming importance of private enterprise in the informal poverty economy cannot be over-emphasized. With only the barest external, public or modern-sector support, it is the private enterprises of the poverty economy that have provided a means of survival, albeit at too rude a level, for a quarter of the human race. This is a tribute to the power of private incentive, individual initiative and the irrepressible dynamism of people, even when oppressed by the burdens that keep them poor. Accordingly, business and professional people everywhere, be they in the First, Second or Third World, should not only be mindful of this fact but be among the first to appreciate that the income and employment generation essential to poverty alleviation must largely be achieved by the private sector. Hence, business and professional people everywhere have the means and the reasons to lobby governments, banks and financial institutions generally to facilitate programmes that seek to help the poor to help themselves. The poor of the world do not need charity nor do they look to charity as the solution to their plight. They wait for a fair go at the resources they need to succeed as entrepreneurs, investors, employers, shopkeepers, artisans and manufacturers.

The process of facilitation open to us as individuals, that will give the poor a fair go at the resources that they can use productively, goes beyond the contribution of one's own time and resources in support of NGOs and CIGPs in particular. Attention has also to be paid to the impact of government policies on the performance of microenterprises in the poverty economy. Private entrepreneurs operate in a macroeconomic environment, whether rich or poor. In the past, however, microenterprise entrepreneurs have been given little or no consideration in the formulation of macroeconomic or industry policies and priorities in the Third World. For example, inflation is by far the worst enemy of the poor. If you have very little money, even a little inflation can quickly take what you have. Yet few developing countries consider their macroeconomic priorities in these terms. It is similar with industry policy. Although we know that firms in a vibrant sector of the economy fare better than those in a stagnant or declining sector, few Third World governments choose economic priorities so as to ensure that the economic cards are stacked in favour of those industries that provide the bulk of the off-farm employment for the poor.

Need for further research
The primary thesis of this book is that there is much that has

133

already been learnt from the pioneers in the CIGP field, and now is the time to imitate their success for the benefit of the poor. I would hope for action to implement the above practical conclusions as soon as possible. This does not imply that there is no need for further research into poverty and its alleviation in developing countries. To the contrary. In particular I would highlight the following:

○ There remains a need to document the progress of the more effective NGOs, especially on a longitudinal basis. The financial viability and sustainability of these programmes need to be assessed and alternative funding strategies explored.

○ How can the commercial banks improve their financial intermediation services to the poor? What role can NGOs play in this process?

○ How can official bilateral aid agencies contribute more effectively to the support of CICGP programmes and NGOs in the Third World?

○ What constraints exist that prevent NGOs from becoming more like a bank, much as the Grameen has done in Bangladesh? Do these same constraints prevent NGOs from acting on behalf of the poor in seeking access to loanable funds from modern-sector financial institutions?

○ What steps must NGOs take if they are to be more effective as sponsors and promoters of CIGPs?

○ How can NGOs and multilateral development agencies, especially the World Bank and the regional development banks, collaborate more productively in their efforts to advance the cause of poverty alleviation in the Third World?

○ What are the most successful programme replication and expansion strategies employed by mature CIGPs? Are these strategies transferable or situation and culture specific?

○ Are there cost-effective ways of identifying a range of profitable investment opportunities for the poor that would not occur to the poor themselves?

Important pilot projects have been initiated by NGOs to examine some of these issues. The variety and potential benefit to the poor of the world from this work is so great, however, that it would be difficult for the international community to over-estimate the value of further empirical research and the practical application of the findings that still lies ahead.

Until quite recently, development for the poor had dropped off the agenda of most developing countries. Consequently, the informal poverty economy has been ignored as a source of development potential and investment opportunities. Yet, the poor are more than a source of cheap labour and sequestered savings; they are demanders of the fruits of development and unsatiated consumers of the output of firms in both modern and traditional industries in the economy. It is in the interests of all those who seek economic development and the alleviation of poverty to put development for the poor back onto the policy agenda in a big way. CIGPs are one effective way in which this agenda can become more than barren rhetoric, and the implementation of the conclusions and recommendations outlined above are some of the practical ways in which this can be done.

Fuelwood gathering for sale. Nepal

Appendix: The Simple Economics of CIGP

The Labour Market

Economists use the simple devices of supply and demand schedules to analyse the performance of markets for commodities and production inputs. We can use these same simple tools of analysis to explore various aspects of the poverty economy and CIGPs in particular. The separate components of the analysis can then be combined to demonstrate the inter-connectedness of the several markets concerned. We begin by examining the labour market as employment generation is the major source of income generation in poor households. Consider Figure A.1.

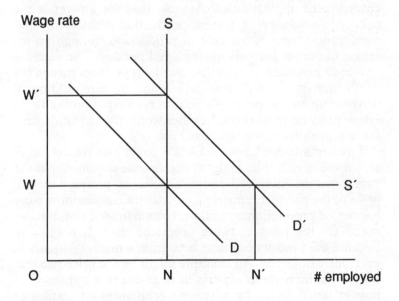

Figure A.1 *Supply and demand for labour*

The downward sloping schedule marked D is the demand curve for labour. It indicates that as the wage rate rises, the demand for labour falls and the number of persons employed also falls. Similarly, as we move down the demand schedule the wage offered to workers falls and demand from employers for labour rises. The supply of labour, on the other hand, can be characterized as a positive relationship between the wage rate available and the amount of labour offered. In the extreme, where the level of unemployment and underemployment is very high, this positive relationship can be represented as an upward sloping schedule that approaches or approximates the horizontal line WS' in Figure A.1. The opposite extreme exists where there is a great scarcity of supply of labour, such as when there is 'over-full employment', and the supply of labour schedule approximates the vertical line SN in Figure A.1. The actual supply schedule will fall somewhere in between these extremes, though in many 'labour surplus' Third World economies the supply-of-labour schedule tends more to the horizontal than to the vertical.

Now consider what happens if at the going wage rate, W dollars per day, there is an increase in demand for labour, from ON to ON'. What might cause such an increase in employment opportunities? Assume that the answer is the sudden availability of a new production technology that significantly reduces the cost of production through an increase in output per person employed per day. The increase in labour productivity that this change represents means the profit-motivated employers will want to hire additional workers up to the point where it is no longer profitable to employ any more workers. In other words the demand curve for labour shifts to the right to D'.

The demand-for-labour schedule could also rise for other reasons. For example, in the above case we assumed that the profit margin increased because costs of production fell, price of the product remaining constant. Consider now what happens if production conditions remain unchanged, but demand for the product being produced rises. It might rise because the product can now be sold in a market which was previously not open. An example might be the price rise that follows an increase in exports in response to a reduction in import tariffs levied by advanced economies on textiles or handicrafts exported from developing countries. In other

138

words, the increase in demand means that more output can be sold at prices no lower than previously obtained in the smaller domestic market, if only additional supplies can be made available. In this situation it becomes profitable for employers to hire extra labour, even though physical output per worker has not increased. It is the 'value' of the output per worker that has increased.

A successful CIGP can be expected to have either or even both of these effects; i.e. an increase in 'productivity' as well as an increase in 'value' in response to a rise in demand. Consequently, in the Figure A.1, the impact of a successful CIGP can be described by a shift in the demand-for-labour schedule from D to D'. At the going wage rate this increase in demand results in an increase in employment of NN'. However, it is unlikely that the supply of labour will be as flexible as this in all circumstances (described by the schedule marked WS'). Imperfections in the labour market will ensure that some of the increase in demand for labour will be absorbed by an increase in the price of labour. In the opposite extreme case, where the available labour supply cannot be increased at all in the short term (described by the schedule marked NS), wages will be driven up by competition by WW' and will remain at the higher level W' so long as the supply of labour did not increase above N. In the real world the actual outcome will settle somewhere between these two extremes.

In economies where unemployment and under-employment are rife there will be a tendency for the impact of CIGPs to be wholly absorbed by changes in the number of persons employed rather than increases in the wage rate. In other words, competition between the unemployed and the underemployed for the rise in demand for labour will tend to compete away any increase in the wage rate as more and more people offer themselves for employment at the going wage rate OW. When the number of people employed reaches ON', the forces of competition are again in balance. Equilibrium is re-established in the labour market, with the demand for labour exactly matched by the supply at the equilibrium wage rate W dollars per day. However, total cash income earned by labour has increased by W(NN').

In summary, the supply and demand for labour diagram above tells us that an income-and-employment-generation project can work either through the supply side with finance

139

of an improvement in the production process, or through the demand side by increasing the demand for the products that are the output of labour's endeavours. In a very real sense, therefore, additional employment is 'derived' from the increased demand for the commodities being produced. Whether the cause of this increase in demand is a fall in price in response to greater efficiency or an increase in the extent of the market being supplied, the aim of a CIGP is to either increase the productivity of labour and thereby the profitability of employing more labour, or to increase the value of the output of labour with a similar consequence for profits and the creation of job opportunities.

The investment market

In a manner similar to that described above for the market for labour, we can explore the market for investment opportunities in order to demonstrate the impact of a CIGP on the cost of capital and the volume of investment activity undertaken by microenterprises. Consider Figure A.2.

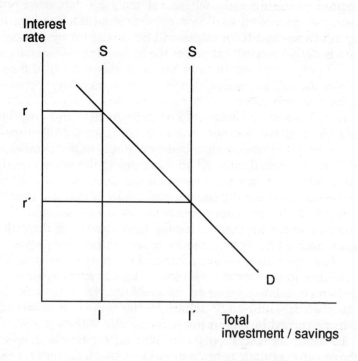

Figure A.2   *Impact of a CIGP on investment and the cost of capital*

On the horizontal axis we show the total value of investments and on the vertical axis the rate of interest or cost of capital. The demand for investment funds is shown as the downward sloping line marked D. It indicates that as the cost of borrowing comes down the demand for investment finance rises. While interest rates are high, only the most profitable investment opportunities can be financed. At lower interests rates it is profitable to finance the less lucrative investment opportunities, so the level of demand for investment finance is greater than at higher interest rates. Once again we see that the demand schedule is negatively sloped, falling from left to right, indicating an inverse relationship between price and quantity.

Consider now the manner in which a traditional informal market for loanable funds might operate. Investment finance is scarce. Bank loans are not available to microentrepreneurs because the banks do not loan to the poor. Banks only loan to those who already have money, or those with tangible assets such as land that can be offered as collateral to underwrite a loan. Consequently, entrepreneurs at each level of the Poverty Pyramid must depend upon personal and family savings, or loans from local moneylenders to finance their working capital, stock holdings, marketing activities or equipment purchases. Both sources, however, do not represent substantial resources. In Figure A.2, assume that the supply of loanable funds is shown by the vertical 'supply-curve' marked S1. At this level of supply of capital only those investment opportunities that are profitable enough to service a loan at the rate of interest r will be viable. The result is an equilibrium between the supply of and demand for loanable funds at the rate of interest r and the level of investment l. This is a high rate of interest and a very low level of investment. Because investment is low, microentrepreneurs being unable to afford the more efficient production methods at the prevailing interest rates, productivity and the flow of value-added from production are also low.

The impact of the CIGP is to raise the available supply of loanable funds for investment finance from S to S′. The increase in supply allows interest rates to fall to r' and the level of investment to rise to l'. ll' of 'additional' investment takes place. This is new investment. CIGPs do not have to seek business by offering to re-finance investments that were profitable at the higher interest rates that previously reigned.

141

By adhering to an 'additionality' principle, the CIGP can maximize its impact on employment and total income produced.

The theory of the 'poverty trap' has as a lemma the notion that 'there are no profitable investment opportunities in the world of the chronically poor'. However, if we accept this piece of received wisdom as true, it remains for us to explain why village-level moneylenders can do business at the rates they are able to charge? The reality is that there are substantial investment opportunities in the 'poverty economy', but there are few that are viable at the very high rates of interest that the denial of credit to the poor sustains. Consider Figure A.3.

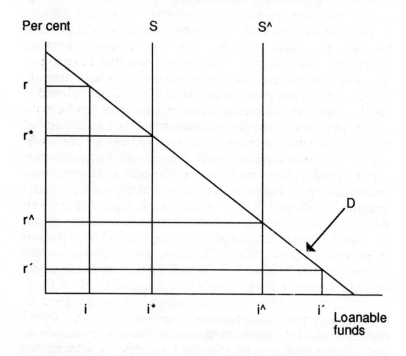

Figure A.3 *Supply and demand for loanable funds*

If one lists in cumulative order the range of investment opportunities available to the poor, as is done in Figure A.3, we find that there are very few investments that offer a very high rate of return, but a much larger number that offer a lower rate of return. In other words, there is a negative relationship between the rate of return available and the number

142

of investment opportunities available at that rate of return. This is saying no more than that there are very many fewer highly profitable projects than the number of not so profitable objects.

This negative relationship is described by the downward sloping schedule marked D in Figure A.3. This is in fact the demand schedule for loanable funds. At the rate of return r%, measured on the vertical axis, there are only $\$i$ of investment opportunities available, measured on the horizontal axis. Hence, at the interest rate r% not more than $\$i$ of investments are profitable enough to service loan financing. However, at the rate of return r'%, there is a much larger volume, $\$i'$, of investment opportunities available that are profitable enough to at least break even at the rate of interest r'%.

The schedule marked D, therefore, describes the demand for finance by potential investors in microenterprises servicing the needs of the poor. The interest rate they have to pay for finance is the critical constraint they face in acting on investment opportunities available to them. The higher that rate is, the lower the volume of investment that can be justified by prospective profits, and vice versa. The actual rate of interest available, however, is determined by the supply of loanable funds relative to demand at any one time.

For the sake of argument let us assume that the amount of loanable funds available is $\$i^{*\prime}$, shown in Figure A.3 by the vertical line marked S. This is the supply-of-loanable-funds schedule. Supply equals demand at the rate of interest r^*. If the supply of finance available to the poor could be increased to S†, let us say as a result of an injection of new credit to microenterprises by an NGO-operated CIGP programme, the rate of interest demanded of poor people would fall to r†, and the level of investment undertaken by the poor would increase to $\$i$†. This higher level of investment is associated with increased employment, plus an increase in productivity and value-added generated within enterprises serving the needs of the poor. Moreover, the increase in investment, $(i^*i$†$)$, has a 'multiplier' effect of substantial proportions as the income generated by the new employment increases consumption demand even further.

Liquidity leakages have an opposite effect to that of a credit injection. If there is a leakage of liquidity, brought on, let us assume, by the introduction of a government-sponsored household small savings mobilization programme, the supply-of-loanable-funds schedule shifts to the left. In Figure A.3 above this would be shown by a shift in the supply curve from S† to S, with the new equilibrium between the demand for loanable funds and the supply settling at a higher rate of interest and a lower level of investment. Hence, the bank deposits of the poor that are not recycled to the poor, and are a leakage that exacerbates the chronic liquidity shortage always facing the poor, make it even more difficult for poor entrepreneurs operating microenterprises to invest and generate jobs than it was before. It is critical, therefore, that if CIGP programmes are to avoid this perverse result of a bank-linked programme, they must obtain guarantees that the co-operating banks will recycle savings deposits by the poor to borrowers from poor households.

The three-sector model
We can complete the story economists tell to link investment credit to income and employment generation in a unique way, through recourse to what we call the 'three quadrant model'. The first part of the quadrant consists of the supply-and-demand-for-loanable-funds schedules that we have just been considering. The second part depicts the relationship between the demand for labour and investment. We assume this to be positive. In other words, if investment, (i), by the poor in microenterprises increases, demand for labour increases and the level of employment, (n), rises. In the third quadrant we establish the link between levels of employment and the level of income, (y), received by the poor. At a given wage rate w, an increase in employment, $(n^*n†)$, results in an increase in income earned, $(y^*y† = w.n^*n†)$. The model is summarized in Figure A.4.

If we begin in equilibrium at the rate of interest i^*, the level of investment, i^*, that can be financed results in a level of employment, n^*, which at the going wage rate, w, generates an income flow to the poor of y^*. After the introduction of a CIGP, the supply of loanable funds increases and a new equilibrium is reached at a lower rate of interest. $r†$. At this lower rate the level of investment that can be financed profitably increases by $i^*i†$, which in turn increases the demand for labour by $n^*n†$. At the going wage rate, w, the increase in employment results in an increase in income received by the poor of $y^*y†$, which equals the increase in employment, $n^*n†$, multiplied by the wage rate, w.

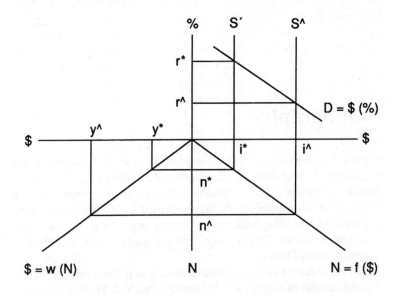

Figure A.4 *The three-quadrant model of income and employment generation*

Bibliography

Acton, Judith (ed.) (1987), *Zimbabwe Project: A Revolving Loan Fund at the Risk End. An Evaluation*, ZPT, Harare.

Akhtar, Shamim (1988), 'Savings and credit programme of the Christian Commission for Development in Bangladesh', paper prepared for the national planning workshop of the Co-operative Credit Union League of Bangladesh Ltd, 2–3 February, mimeo, Dhaka.

Anderson, Dennis (1982), 'Small industry in developing countries: a discussion of issues', *World Development*, Vol. 10, No. 11: 913–48.

Anderson, Dennis and Farida Khambata (1985), 'Financing small-scale industry and agriculture in developing countries: the merits and limitations of "commercial" policies', *Economic Development and Cultural Change*, Vol. 2 (January): 349–71.

Annis, Sheldon, 'The shifting grounds of poverty lending at the World Bank', mimeo, pp. 87–109.

Annis, Sheldon and Peter Hakim (1988), *Direct to the Poor: Grassroots Development in Latin America*, Lynne Rienner, Boulder.

Anon (1985), *The Role of Rural Credit in Reaching the Poor: IFAD's Experience*, IFAD special studies series, Tycooly Publishing, Oxford.

Anon (1988a), 'Zimbabwe Project and collective co-operatives: an overview of rural credit and the revolving loan fund', mimeo, Harare.

Anon (1988b) 'Sarvodaya economic enterprises development services', paper presented at NOVIB, Netherlands pre-donor consortium meeting, 4–5 February, mimeo, Colombo.

Ashe, Jeffrey (1985a), *The Pisces II Experience, Vol. 1: Local efforts in microenterprise development*, USAID, Washington DC.

Ashe, Jeffrey (ed.) (1985b), *The Pisces II Experience, Vol. 2: Local efforts in microenterprise development: case studies from Dominican*

Republic, Costa Rica, Kenya and Egypt, USAID, Washington DC.

Asian Development Bank (ADB) (1987), *The Bank's Cooperation with Non-governmental Organizations*, Board Paper ·R79–87, Development Policy Office, ADB, Manila.

Bigelow, Ross E., Cotter, Jim, Nbajah, Esther M., and Ondeng, Peter G. (1987) 'Mid-term evaluation of the Rural Enterprise Programme of the Rural Private Enterprise Project (615–0220)', a report prepared for the USAID Mission, mimeo, Nairobi, Kenya.

Biggs, Tyler and Oppenheim, Jeremy (1986), 'What drives the size distribution of firms in developing countries?', EEPA Discussion Paper No. 6, mimeo, Employment and Small Enterprise Division, Bureau of Science and Technology, USAID, Grant DAN–5426–C–00–4098–0.

Blayney, Robert G. and Otero, Maria (1985), *Small and Micro-enterprises: Contributions to Support*, USAID, Washington DC.

Bolnick, Bruce, R. (1982), 'Concessional credit for small scale enterprise', *Bulletin of Indonesian Economic Studies*, Vol. 18, No. 2 (July):65–85.

Bolnick, Bruce R. (1987) 'Financial liberalization with imperfect markets: Indonesia during the 1970s', *Economic Development and Cultural Change* (April): 581–99.

BRAC (1987), *Mid-year Report: Rural Development Programme*, BRAC, mimeo, Dhaka.

Bysouth, Kaye A. (ed.) (1986), *The Positive Development Programme*, Community Aid Abroad, Melbourne.

Callanta, Ruth S. (1987), *Institutional Strategy of the Philippines Business for Social Progress, 1986–91*, PBSP, Manila.

Carr, Marilyn (1988), 'Institutional aspects of microenterprise promotion', paper presented at the World Conference on 'Support of microenterprises' of Committee of Donor Agencies for Small Enterprise Development, 6–9 June, Washington DC.

CCDB Study Team (1987), *Report on the CCDB Savings and Credit Programme*, CCDB, Dhaka.

Cernea, Michael M. (1987), 'Farmer organizations and institution building for sustainable development', *Regional Development Dialogue*, Vol. 8, No. 2: 1–19.

Chandavarkar, Anand G. (1988), 'The role of informal credit markets in support of microbusinesses in developing countries', paper presented at the World Conference on 'Support of microenterprises' of Committee of Donor Agencies for Small Enterprise Development, 6–9 June, Washington DC.

Cookingham, Frank (1988), 'The floods have wiped them out', *Together* (January–March):12–13.

Croucher, Jack and Gupta, S.K. (1988), 'Venture capital for microenterprise development: the VCAT model', paper presented at the World Conference on 'Support of microenterprises' of Committee of Donor Agencies for Small Enterprise Development, 6–9 June, Washington DC.

Dasgupta, Subhachari (1987), *Towards Alternative Banking: Review of Indian Experience*, People's Institute for Development and Training, New Delhi.

de Chavez, Marites D., Laforteza, Emma C. and Imperial, Antonio C. (1987), 'Investing in the urban poor: the Metro Manila livelihood programme', Occasional Paper No. 3, PBSP, Manila.

de Soto, Hernando (1987), 'Constraints on people: the origins of underground economies and limits to their growth', a book review of *El Otro Sendero* (The Other Path), Instituto Libertad y Democracia (ILD), Lima, Peru.

Drabek, Anne Gordon (1987), 'Development alternatives: the challenge for NGOs — an overview of the issues', *World Development*, Vol. 15, Supplement: ix–xv.

Ekanayake, Ariyapala and Hettiarachchi, Ranjith (eds) (1986), *Thrift and Credit Cooperative Societies Movement — Sri Lanka*, Centre for Development Communications, Monograph No. 3, Colombo.

Elliott, Charles (1987), *Comfortable Compassion*, Hodder & Stoughton, London.

Else, John (1987), *NGO Activities in Income Generating Projects (IGPs) in Zimbabwe*, VOICE, Harare.

Emecheta, Buchi (1979), *The Joys of Motherhood*, Allison & Busby, London.

Farbman, Michael (ed.) (1981), *The Pisces Studies: Assisting the Smallest Economic Activities of the Poor*, Office of Urban Development, Bureau for Science and Technology, USAID, Washington DC, September.

Farnsworth, Clyde H. (1988), 'Micro-loans to the world's poorest', *New York Times*, 21 February.

Fass, Simon (1980), *The Economics of Survival: A Study of Poverty and Planning in Haiti*, USAID, Office of Urban Development, Washington DC.

Fernando, B. (1986), 'Revolving loan field report', WVSL, mimeo, Columbo.

Finny, Matthew and Sujeevandas (1988), 'India: partnership with the poor', *Together* (January–March): 8–10.

Fonstad, Carmenza *et al.* (1982), *Pisces: The Smallest Businesses of the Poor: An Annotated Bibliography*, ACCION International/ AITEC, Cambridge MA 02138.

Fuglesang, Andreas and Chandler, Dale (1986), *Participation as Process: What We Can Learn from Grameen Bank, Bangladesh*, NORAD, Oslo.

Graber, Glen D. (1988), 'Credit for the poor: are revolving loans the answer?', *Together* (January–March):1–2.

Guigu, George M., Alila, Patrick O., Mwabu, Germano M. (1987), 'The development of women entrepreneurship: an evaluation of Partnership for Productivity/Kenya (PfP) women in development project', consulting report to PfP/Kenya, mimeo, Nairobi.

Harper, Malcolm (1984), *Small Business in the Third World*, John Wiley & Sons, Chichester.

Harper, Malcolm (1988), 'Training and technical assistance for microenterprise', paper presented at the World Conference on 'Support of microenterprises' of Committee of Donor Agencies for Small Enterprise Development, 6–9 June, Washington DC.

Harper, Malcolm and Soon, Tan Thiam (1979), *Small Enterprises in Developing Countries*, IT Publications, London.

Hatch, John K. (1988), 'Suggestions for implementing the new Microenterprise Act: presenting a generic model for village banking programme', mimeo, FIMCA, Tucson, Arizona (March):18 + append. a–d.

Hellinger, Stephen, Hellinger, Douglas and O'Regan, Fred M. (1988), *Aid for Just Development*, Lynne Rienner Pub. Inc., Boulder, Colorado.

Holdcroft, Lane E. (1984), 'The rise and fall of community development, 1950–65: a critical assessment', in J. M. Staatz and C. K. Eicher (eds), *Agricultural Development in the Third World*, Johns Hopkins UP, Baltimore, pp. 46–58.

Hossain, Mahabub (1984), *Credit for the Rural Poor: The Experience of Grameen Bank in Bangladesh*, Bangladesh Institute of Development Studies, Dhaka.

Hunt, Robert W. and Mirero, S. M. A. (1985), *End of Project Evaluation of the Small Business Scheme of the National Christian Council of Kenya*, USAID, Purchase Order No. DAN-1096-0-4046 (March), Washington DC.

Hutchinson, Judy (1984), 'Special evaluation of World Vision Sri Lanka revolving loan programme', World Vision interoffice memo, 6 September, Los Angeles.

IIDI (1987), *Jeeva Sanwardhanaya Ayathanaya Pilot Year Evaluation, 1986 and Programme Projections, 1987*, IIDI/JSA, Chicago.

IIDI (1987), *Annual Report* (May), Elmhurst, Il 60126, USA.

Indian Planning Commission (1965), *The Second Five Year Plan*, Government of India, New Delhi.

Jackelen, Henry R. (1988) 'Banking on the informal sector: suggestions on using financial institutions to reach microenterprises in developing countries', paper presented at the World Conference on 'Support of microenterprises' of Committee of Donor Agencies for Small Enterprise Development, 6–9 June, Washington DC.

Jacobi, Norton (1988), 'Loan principles that have worked in Sri Lanka', *Together* (January–March): 7.

Kahnert, Friedrich (1987), 'Improving urban employment and labor productivity', World Bank Discussion Paper No. 10, Washington DC.

Korten, David C. (1980), 'Community organization and rural development: a learning process approach', *Public Administration Review* (Sept./Oct.): 480–511.

Korten, David C. (1987), 'Third generation NGO strategies: a key to people-centered development', *World Development*, Vol. 15, Supplement: 145–59.

Korten, David C. (1988), *NGOs and The Future of Asian Development*, Institute for Development Research, Boston (April).

Korten, David C. (1989), 'The US voluntary sector and global realities: issues for the 1990s', *USAID Issues Paper*, mimeo, Institute for Development Research, Washington DC.

KREP (1985), 'NCCK small business scheme, six-month bridging grant, project summary', mimeo, Nairobi.

Lapierre, Dominique (1986), *The City of Joy*, Century Hutchinson Ltd, London.

Levitsky, Jacob (1986), *World Bank Lending to Small Enterprises: A Review*, Industry and Finance Series, Vol. 16, The World Bank, Washington DC.

Levitsky, Jacob (1988), 'Summary Report: World Conference on Microenterprises', Committee of Donor Agencies for Small Enterprise Development, Secretariat, World Bank Bldg, Room N–9033, Washington DC.

Levitsky, Jacob and Prasad, Ranga N. (1987), 'Credit guarantee schemes for small and medium enterprises', World Bank Technical Paper No. 58, Industry and Finance Series, Washington DC.

Liedholm, Carl and Mead, Donald (1987), 'Small-scale industries in developing countries: empirical evidence and policy implications', MSU International Development Paper No. 9, report to USAID from Department of Agricultural Economics, Michigan State University, under contract number DAN–1090–A–00–2087–00.

Lipton, Michael (1988), 'The poor and the poorest', World Bank Discussion Paper No. 25, World Bank, Washington DC.

Mahalanobis, P. C. (1963) *The Approach of Operational Research to Planning in India*, Indian Statistical Institute, Bombay.

Mann, Charles K., Grindle, Merilee S. and Shrimpton, Parker (eds) (1989), *Seeking Solutions: Framework and Cases for Small Enterprise Development Programme*, Kumarian Press, Connecticut.

Mapondera, E. N. (1986), *Zimbabwe Women's Bureau: Programme and Projects*, ZWB, Harare.

Markandaya, Kamala (1954), *Nectar in a Sieve*, John Day, New York.

Mazumdar, Dipak (1976), 'The urban informal sector', *World Development*, 4(8):655–79.

McGinnis, Linda (1988), 'Evaluation of the Kenya Commercial Bank informal sector Jua Kali loan programme (a pilot scheme)', Evaluation Report No. 1, USAID/Kenya, Raj Bhatia, Investment Promotion Centre, Nairobi.

Meyer, Richard L. (1988), 'Financial services for microenterprises: programme or markets?', paper presented at the World Conference on 'Support of microenterprises' of Committee of Donor Agencies for Small Enterprise Development (June 6–9), Washington DC.

Moloney, Clarence (1985), *Report on NGO Programme in Rural Savings and Credit in Bangladesh*, Robert Nathan Associates and S. F. Ahmed & Co., Dhaka.

OECD (1988), *Voluntary Aid for Development: The Role of Non-government Organizations*, OECD, Paris.

Otero, Maria (1988), 'Microenterprise assistance programmes: their benefits, costs and sustainability', paper presented at the World Conference on 'Support of microenterprises' of Committee of Donor Agencies for Small Enterprise Development (June 6–9), Washington DC.

Ramenaden, Philip and Berman, Noel (1988), 'Credit for the poor in Sri Lanka', *Together* (January–March): 5–7.

Rao, C. R. *et al.* (eds) (1963), *Essays on Econometrics and Planning*, Permagon Press, Calcutta.

151

Remenyi, Joe (1990), 'Food, population and the environment', *New Horizons in Education*, No. 82, June, pp. 212–20.

Riungu, D. N. and Nzioki, B. K. (1986), 'Executive summary: Daraja Trust Co. Ltd: evaluation of existing projects and area need assessment survey, Vol. 1', consultants' report, mimeo, Nairobi.

Schneider, Bertrand (1988a), *The Barefoot Revolution*, a report to the Club of Rome, IT Publications, London.

Schneider, Bertrand (1988b), 'Can NGOs, PVOs and local initiatives for development of the poorest southern countries help eradicate famine and malnutrition?', paper presented at the World Conference on 'Support of microenterprises' of Committee of Donor Agencies for Small Enterprise Development (June 6–9), Washington DC.

Sebstad, Jennefer (1982), *Struggle and Development Among Self Employed Women*, a report on the Self-employed Women's Association, Ahmedabad, India, USAID, Bureau for Science and Technology, Office of Urban Development, Contract No. OTR–1406–C–00–1004–00, Washington DC.

Seibel, Hans Deiter (1988), 'Financial innovations for microenterprises: linking informal and formal financial institutions in Africa and Asia', paper presented at the World Conference on 'Support of microenterprises' of Committee of Donor Agencies for Small Enterprise Development (June 6–9), Washington DC.

Sen, Amartya (1980), 'Levels of poverty: policy and change', World Bank staff working paper No. 401, World Bank, Washington DC.

Sen, Amartya (1981), *Poverty and Famines: An Essay on Entitlement and Deprivation*, Clarendon Press, Oxford.

Sethuraman, S. V. (ed.) (1981), *The Urban Informal Sector in Developing Countries*, ILO, Geneva.

Swincer, Graeme (1988), 'Lessons learned in revolving loan funds', *Together* (January–March): 11–12.

Tendler, Judith (1987), *Whatever Happened to Poverty Alleviation?*, a report prepared for the mid-decade review of the Ford Foundation's programme on Livelihood, Employment, and Income Generation, Ford Foundation, New York.

Timberg, Thomas A. (1988), 'Comparative experience with microenterprise projects', paper presented at the World Conference on 'Support of microenterprises' of Committee of Donor Agencies for Small Enterprise Development (June 6–9), Washington DC.

Tripatsas, George, Crichlow, Brooks and Gnanakuru, Chandran, (1987), 'Small and micro-enterprise development in Africa', John F. Kennedy School of Government, Harvard University, and IIDI, mimeo, Boston.

USAID (1985), Searching for benefits', AID Evaluation Special Study No. 28, PN–AAL–056 (June), USAID, Washington DC.

Van Leeuwen, R., Passtoors, W. and Wils, F. (1987), 'Netherlands multidisciplinary team assessment of BRAC', NOVIB/BRAC, mimeo, Dhaka.

WCCU (1987), 'Bangladesh feasibility study report', CULB, mimeo, Dhaka.

Wijayapala, Lal and Gamage, Cyril (1986), 'Thrift and credit co-operative societies: Sri Lanka experience', TCCS/CAA Evaluation, Columbo.

Wilkinson, Betty (1985), 'Evaluation of savings and credit in rural Bangladesh: experiences of small credit schemes', Oxfam consultancy report, unpublished mimeo.

Williams, Homer (ed.) (1986), *Diversity in Development*, Inter Action, New York.

World Bank (1978), 'Employment and development of small enterprises', Sector Policy Paper, Washington DC.

Yunus, Mohammad (1987a), *Credit for Self-employment: A Fundamental Human Right*, Grameen Bank, Dhaka.

Yunus, Mohammad (1987b), 'The poor as the engine of development', *The Washington Quarterly*, 10(4), Autumn.

Yunus, Mohammad (1988), 'Grameen Bank: organisation and operations', paper presented at the World Conference on 'Support of microenterprises' of Committee of Donor Agencies for Small Enterprise Development (June 6–9), Washington DC.

153

Acronyms

ACCION INT'L.	Americans for Community Co-operation in Other Nations
ADAB	Association of Development Agencies in Bangladesh
AFFHC*	Australian Freedom from Hunger Campaign
AIDAB*	Australian International Development Assistance Bureau
AVARD	Association of Voluntary Agencies for Rural Development (India)
BfdW	Bread for the World, W. Germany
BKK	Badan Kredit Kecamatan, Indonesia
BRAC*	Bangladesh Rural Advancement Committee
CARE Inc.	formerly Cooperative for American Relief Everywhere
CCDB*	Christian Commission for Development in Bangladesh
CD	Community Development
CEOSS	Coptic Evangelical Organization for Social Services
CIGP	Credit-based income-generation project
CRTD	Centre for Rural Technology Development (Philippines, sponsored by PBSP, also offers training)
CULB*	Credit Union League of Bangladesh
DGap	Development Group for Alternative Policies, (subcontractor in the PISCES project)
DMCS*	Dondolo Mudonzvo Credit Society, Zimbabwe
DRI	Differential Rate of Interest, India
DST*	Divya Shanti Trust, Bangalore, India
DTCL*	Daraja Trust Company Ltd, Kenya
EZE*	Evangelische Zentralstelle fur Entwicklungshifle, W. Germany

154

EMW	Evangelisches Missionswerk (Protestant Association for World Mission)
FFHF	Freedom from Hunger Foundation
FINCA	Foundation for International Community Assistance
GNP	Gross National Product
IDB	Inter-American Development Bank (also referred to as IADB)
IDH	Instituto para el Desarrollo Hondureno (Institute for Honduran Development)
IFAD	International Fund for Agricultural Development
IFDA	International Federation for Another Development (Nyon, Switzerland)
IGP	Income-Generation Project/Programme
IIDI*	Institute for International Development, Inc. (Chicago)
IRDP	Interest Rate Differential Programme, India
IIRR	International Institute of Rural Reconstruction, Philippines
JSA*	Jeeva Sanwardhanaya Ayathanaya, Sri Lanka
KICB Jua Kali	Kenya Commercial Bank Small Loan Programme
KREP*	Kenya Rural Enterprise Programme
MBM*	Maha Bhoga Marga, Bali, Indonesia (Bridge to Progress)
MEDA	Menonite Economic Development Associates
MIDAS	Microenterprise Development Assistance Scheme (USAID)- funded programme in Bangladesh)
MMLP*	Metro Manila Livelihood Programme, PBSP
NCCB	National Council of Churches of Bangladesh
NCCK*	National Council of Churches of Kenya
NGO	Non-Governmental Organization
OEFI	Overseas Education Fund International
OI	Opportunity International (formerly IIDI)
OPIC	Overseas Private Investment Corporation (US based PVO)
OXFAM	Oxford Committee for Famine Relief (UK based)
PACT	Private Agencies Collaborating Together (US based)
PBSP*	Philippines Business for Social Progress
PfPZ*	Partnership for Productivity, Zimbabwe
PISCES	Programme for Investment in the Small Capital Enterprise Sector

REAL	Reconstruction through Education, Action and Leadership (Tamil Nadu, India)
SCF	Save the Children Fund
SEDCO*	Small Enterprise Development Corporation, Zimbabwe
SEWA	Self-Employed Women's Association, Ahmadabad, India
TARD	Technical Assistance for Rural Development, Bangladesh
TBF*	The Bridge Foundation, India
TCCS Ltd	Thrift and Credit Cooperative Societies Ltd, Sri Lanka
TSPI*	Tulay Sa Pag-Unlad, Inc., Philippines (Bridge to Progress)
UNDP	United Nations Development Programme
USAID*	United States Agency for International Development, Washington DC 20523
VOICE*	Voluntary Organizations in Community Enterprise, Harare, Zimbabwe
WCC	World Council of Churches
WCCU	World Council of Credit Unions
WWF	Working Women's Forum, Madras, India
YIS*	Yayasan Indonesia Sejahtera, Solo, Indonesia (Indonesian Welfare Foundation)
ZPT*	Zimbabwe Project Trust
ZWB*	Zimbabwe Women's Bureau
ZWBP*	Zimbabwe Women's Banking Project

*Projects visited for this study.